Can you just imagine the visiting, the stories, and the fellowship that have gone on during the making of all the wonderful quilts through the years? And can you imagine all the children who have been tucked in securely underneath them in their beds night after night? And us adults too?

That's what you call "comfort from a country quilt." I hope this book is as comforting to you as my mama's quilt has always been to me. Like a quilt, this book is made up of small pieces of material—some of my favorite stories, memorable experiences, and more than a few opinions—written, rather than sewn, from the stuff of my life. I have stitched these pieces together with my sincere hope that you will find this "quilt" of a book friendly, warm, and enjoyable, something you can turn to for comfort and entertainment and for sharing with friends and family.

Also published by Bantam Books

REBA: MY STORY

by Reba McEntire

with Tom Carter

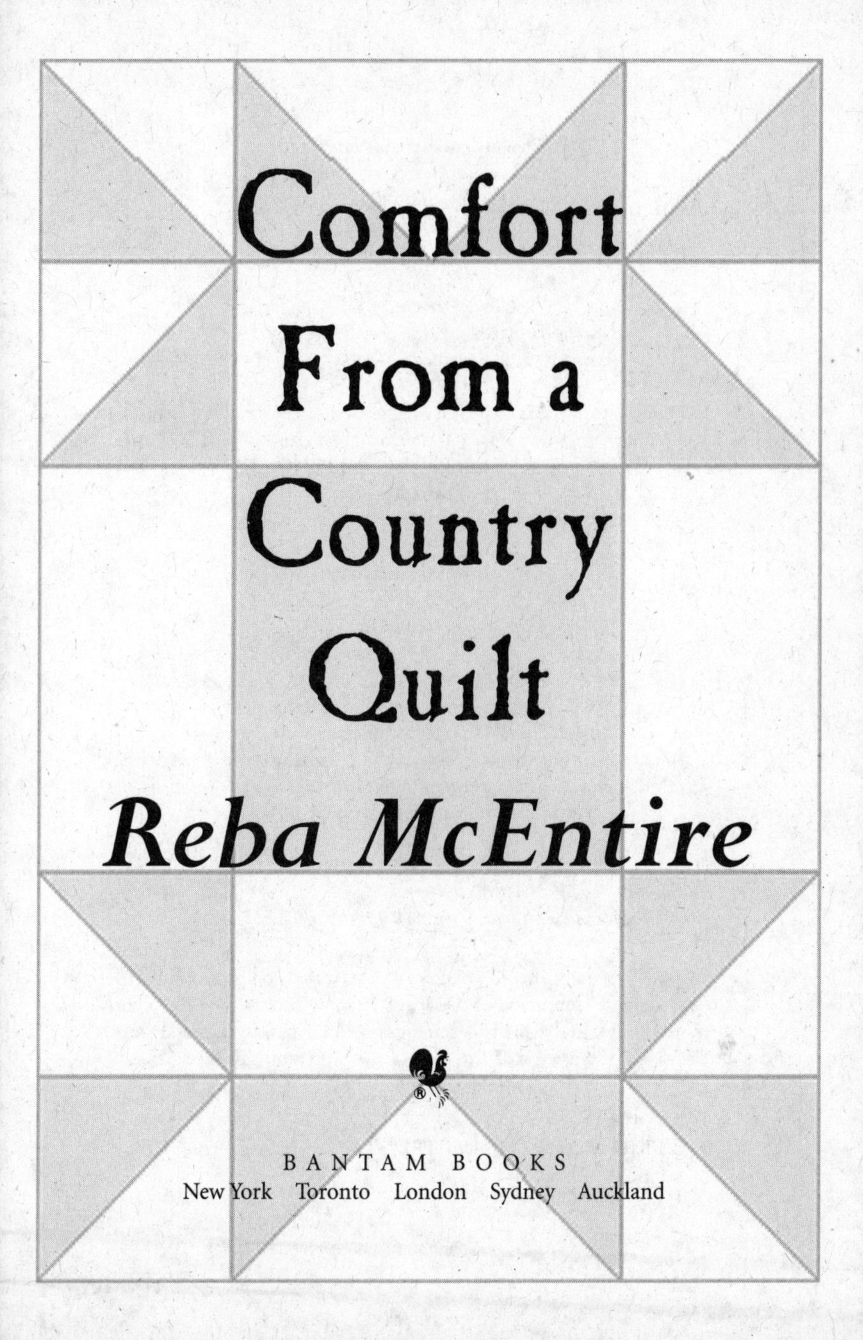

Comfort From a Country Quilt

Reba McEntire

BANTAM BOOKS
New York Toronto London Sydney Auckland

This edition contains the complete text
of the original hardcover edition.
NOT ONE WORD HAS BEEN OMITTED.

COMFORT FROM A COUNTRY QUILT

PUBLISHING HISTORY
Bantam hardcover edition published May 1999
Bantam trade paperback edition / May 2000

Grateful acknowledgment is made for permission to quote from
"I Know I'll Have a Better Day Tomorrow." Written by Reba McEntire.

Library of Congress Catalog Card Number: 99-21644.

ISBN 0-553-38094-X

Published simultaneously in the United States and Canada

Bantam Books are published by Bantam Books, a division of Random House, Inc. Its trademark, consisting of the words "Bantam Books" and the portrayal of a rooster, is Registered in U.S. Patent and Trademark Office and in other countries. Marca Registrada. Bantam Books, 1540 Broadway, New York, New York 10036.

PRINTED IN THE UNITED STATES OF AMERICA

RRH 10 9 8 7 6 5 4 3 2

I dedicate this book to those who love a good story, whether it's funny, sad, educational, or just one to snuggle up with.

If you want to make God laugh,
just tell Him your plans.

—Minnie Pearl

Contents

Acknowledgments

I appreciate all the time and places I have gotten to write this book, backstage in dressing rooms, in-flight to the next show, and back home again. It was interesting and fun. And it sure beat just sitting on the plane or in the dressing rooms letting Sandi, my stylist, beat me at cards one more time!

To Irwyn Applebaum, thank you for being my editor, encourager, idea man, and go-between! You're great to work with.

To Narvel Blackstock, thank you for keeping me focused and reminding me of all the fun and great things we've gotten to do together so I could write about them.

To Mama, Daddy, Alice, Pake, and Susie, thanks for helping me to remember all the fun we had growing up in Oklahoma and all the miles we covered together!

To Shelby: You will always be my favorite subject

to write about. Thanks for the best material a writer could wish for!

To my Heavenly Father: You have blessed me beyond my wildest dreams. Thank you for letting me write down all these many memories you've let me have. Your love embraces me like the comfort from a country quilt.

Comfort From a Country Quilt

Have you ever made a quilt? I have. It's one of the most therapeutic and calming things I've ever done. And I had a huge sense of accomplishment when I finished.

Both of my grandmothers made quilts, my mama did, and my aunt Jeannie did. I loved to open that big box at Christmastime knowing it was a quilt that one of them had made. I was so flattered that after all the time and energy they had spent on that quilt, they had selected me to receive it. Even as a young girl, I knew a quilt was a gift I would cherish always.

Back when I was living at home, I remember during the winter months Mama would set up her sewing machine in the living room over by the window. At night when we'd all be in there watching TV after supper, Mama would be over at her sewing machine, making another quilt from the scraps left over from a dress or blouse she had made for one of us earlier.

Then, when she had all the squares sewn together, she'd lay the batting on the living room floor, lay the quilted piece on top of that, and then start tacking it down. When that was completed, she'd sew the border around it. Then it was finished. All that remained was for Mama to decide who would be the proud recipient of her precious handiwork which represented so many hours of love.

I feel very blessed to have received one of Mama's quilts. I sleep under it every night I'm home. It doesn't match the fancy comforter we bought in Los Angeles, but it feels better than anything you can imagine. Just because I know my mama made it just for me.

When Daddy's mother died in 1950, one year before my sister Alice was born, Mama got the trunk that held all of the quilts, china, crystal, silverware, and knickknacks that Grandma had collected during her lifetime. Mama discovered that Grandma's trunk also included a few quilt pieces that she had started but had never finished. My sister Susie eventually wound up with those quilt pieces and we all figured she would finish them out and keep them for herself.

But as only Susie would do, she cut the makings of the quilt into four squares, had them quilted, put a picture of Grandma McEntire and a description of the quilt together, and had them framed for Alice's, my brother Pake's, and my Christmas present.

That's how thoughtful Susie is. She could have kept the quilt for herself, but, instead, she shared with her brother and sisters something so special, which had belonged to a woman none of us had ever met. That's part of Susie's charm.

That's also the charm of a quilt. Like a mother, it wraps its arms around you—so soft, yet so sturdy, and so comforting. In my grandma's time the sewing of a quilt would bring friends and neighbors together, and in quilting circles today that lovely tradition continues. Now we live in a time when so many women do not even have a sewing machine in their home and when country quilts hang in the fanciest boutiques and galleries selling as "decorative art." That would sure give my grandma and her circle a good laugh and more than a few shakes of the head.

Can you just imagine the visiting, the stories, and the fellowship that have gone on during the making of all the wonderful quilts through the years? And can you imagine all the children who have been tucked in securely underneath them in their beds night after night? And us adults too?

That's what you call "comfort from a country quilt." I hope this book is as comforting to you as my mama's quilt has always been to me. Like a quilt, this book is made up of small pieces of material—some of my favorite stories, memorable experiences, and more than a few opinions—written, rather than sewn, from the stuff of my life. I have stitched these pieces together with my sincere hope that you will find this "quilt" of a book friendly, warm, and enjoyable, something you can turn to for comfort and entertainment and for sharing with friends and family.

So grab your favorite quilt, wrap up, get comfortable, and enjoy.

From me to you.

Love,

Reba

Proud to Be a Modern Country Woman

W*hen Loretta Lynn first sang* "I'm proud to be a coal miner's daughter," she created one of the simplest, boldest, most memorable statements anybody has ever made in any kind of music. It's very important for everyone to be proud of his or her heritage. There's no question how Loretta feels about her heritage.

And there's no question how I feel about mine!

I'm not only proud of my McEntire family heritage and all the things the members of that family have accomplished, I have the utmost respect for the backgrounds of all people. It is my happy experience that country music fans are an absolute melting pot of the American people. We come from all over geographically and from all walks of life.

But I do have a soft spot in my heart for those of us

who grew up far from any decent-sized cities, or even any bustling suburbs, the ones who grew up in the "country."

No matter what our backgrounds are, we're all living in a modern world and trying our best to cope with its challenges. Somehow, facing all the stress and change that our lives consist of these days is easier for those of us who can still draw guidance, experience, and strength from our heritage.

Countless times in each day, I find myself drawing from some family experience, or some bit of wisdom I've learned along the way, to help me confront the twenty-first century crises in my hectic personal and professional life. We all know by now that we can't have it all in life, but I'm convinced I would have a whole lot less if I went through my days without the bounty I carry forward from my heritage.

So, here's to the modern country woman:

She graduated college but finds her country wisdom gets her through more often than her degree.

She can take meetings on the front line all day long but longs for an all-day hike in the backwoods.

She knows the difference between bluepoint oysters and mountain oysters.

She can enjoy herself on Broadway or at the speedway.

She is as comfortable helping her little one explore

a spider's web as she is helping him surf the World Wide Web.

She can kick back at the country fair, then kick off her shoes and read *Vanity Fair.*

She could have an exciting afternoon at either the rodeo or on Rodeo Drive.

Whether you're a *modern country woman* or just a *modern woman,* women have a lot in common. We're versatile, strong, affectionate, opinionated, lovable, and very proud of where we've come from. Aren't we the lucky ones!

As Close as You Can

T*o some people, it's not a* big deal to be with family, but it's always been a big deal for the McEntires to be together. Mama and Daddy started out with just each other, in the same hills of Oklahoma where they themselves grew up and where their own parents still lived. They added four kids—my sister Alice, my brother, Pake, yours truly, and my sister Susie—and they acquired a working cattle ranch that was our school and our playground.

Land is one of the other things that meant everything to our family. Whenever Daddy could put together any winnings at the rodeo, he would buy another parcel of land in our beloved Oklahoma. It's ironic that the bigger our spread, the closer we became, in no small part because there was that much more for us to work on—together.

When we were growing up, we could have been the poster family to show how the family that works—and works and works and works—together stays together. Sometimes we carried that to extremes, like when we would have to stay overnight at a motel on the road between rodeos. All six of us stayed in one room, with two double beds. That meant Mama and Daddy in one bed, Alice, Susie, and me in the other one, and Pake usually got the bathtub, because there was rarely a sofa in the room or one big enough for him to sleep on. It was close, but to us, comfort was not a substitute for sticking together. Plus, with money always being tight, there were not a lot of options.

A close family like ours also keeps anyone's ego from taking up too much room. Alice always says, "Reba is just like anyone else, she just sings a little better than most of us." I would be perfectly happy if my tombstone read *Reba loved life to the fullest! She was a very nice and friendly person.*

One of my greatest joys of the last several years is that my husband, Narvel, and I have welcomed his children from his first marriage into our home and our lives in a way that has expanded our family in wonderful—and noisy—ways.

Shawna, now twenty-five, is Narvel's eldest daughter. She is married to Harley Reed and they have a beautiful five-year-old daughter named Chelsea.

Brandon, twenty-two, is Narvel's son, and Chassidy, twenty, is Narvel's youngest daughter. They all live close by us.

It's so great for Narvel's and my son, Shelby, to be surrounded by family the way I was, and it gives me more of the most rewarding of family memories even though now and then are totally different!

Mama

I*'ve always been proud to be* a redhead, mainly because my mama is one.

Jacqueline Smith McEntire was born on November 6, 1927, a sharecropper's daughter. She was a schoolteacher and has always been a strong woman. I told her once that in my next life I wanted to come back as a man because I always thought men had it easier than us girls did. She laughed and said, "Honey, I've wished that I was a man all my life." She might as well have been a man. She did a man's work *and* a woman's work.

This was business as usual for ranch women, something I learned early on, when I had to go up to the house to help prepare the noon meal, serve it, clean up, and then go right back out again to work beside my brother and father, neither of whom helped out during the meal except to help themselves to more food. This was customary to those times. The women worked inside the house, raised and took care of the children, and still were expected to help with the outside work.

Alice, Susie, and I never knew anything different. It's still pretty much the same today. I guess that's where the saying "It's a man's world" comes from.

Mama and Daddy knew each other for a number of years before they ever dated. Daddy recalls: "I was a little ol' bashful, heavyset boy and I didn't pay much attention to girls. One day I went to Jackie's house and I saw she was carrying two five-gallon buckets full of water to her daddy's hogs. I thought, say, she might fit in to my business plans just fine since it seemed she liked to work."

All right, it's not a courtship story torn from the old *Ranch Romance* pulp magazines, but in 1950 they got married. Daddy is fond of teasing: "My daddy always told me there were three things a man didn't need: a roguish sow, a fence-breaking cow, and a redheaded woman, and I wound up with all three of them!"

And if Mama's within earshot, she'll fire back without skipping a beat, "And you've enjoyed every minute of it."

For her part, Mama will admit that "I always knew that I wanted children and I wanted my husband to be someone I thought would be a good father, who would make the breed a little better, and I think I got him." They didn't take long to get started either. My sister Alice, my brother, Pake, and I were each born about eighteen months apart, and our baby sister, Susie, is only two years younger than me. Yes, Mama had four kids under the age of six by 1957! Daddy was rodeoing as much as he could, so he wasn't around that much to help her.

After all of us kids grew up and moved away from the homeplace, Mama became Daddy's right-hand hired hand! I guess you can't feel guilty about getting married and leaving home. It's meant to be—it says so in the Bible. But I always did feel guilty when I saw how hard Mama and Daddy continued to work.

One time Mama and Daddy were down at the pens working cattle. Daddy was at the chute branding, worming, and vaccinating the cattle, while Mama would get behind the cattle back in the alleyway and bring an amount that the smaller holding pen could handle and pull the so-called panel gate shut behind them.

That day there was a big ol' gray Brahma steer that wanted to be anywhere on earth but there in those pens. So, when Mama got behind him and he ran into the smaller pen, he changed his mind about his location immediately! By the time Mama got the panel gate closed, he was running straight toward her with a full head of steam! Mama was on the opposite side of the panel gate, so when he hit the panel it was knocked off its hinges into and on top of Mama.

Then the big ol' Brahma proceeded to walk along the panel—and Mama—as if it were a foot log. She got three broken ribs from that incident. But did Mama get up and go to the house? Oh, no. They finished up and headed out. I think an Ace bandage was the only medical treatment she allowed herself until they got through with their chore. Only then did she go to the doctor.

One afternoon Mama and Daddy were at the pens, doctoring some cattle, and Mama was walking from the chute back to the pens to get another bunch of cattle. As almost every one of us had done before, Mama hit her head on the board that was just forehead level, above the walk-through. She was concentrating on her mission, so she hit that board pretty hard.

Daddy looked over at her to see if she was okay. She didn't say a word. She climbed over the fence, went to the house, and got the chain saw. When she returned, she told Daddy to "cut the sonofabitch down!" He cut it down, and that was the last time anyone got knocked out by that notorious board.

Not only was Mama a good hand on the ranch, she was also a great cook and referee. In the late afternoon after school, Pake, Susie, and I would get in the living room and practice our singing. We were, by this time, The Singing McEntires. Thanks in large part to Mama's perseverance, our school had a country music band, The Kiowa High School Cowboy Band.

Inevitably, one of us would get to arguing about who was singing on whose part and getting mad if someone hadn't done their homework in memorizing the words to a song. Mama would be in the kitchen fixing supper, and after listening to all she could stand of our arguing, she'd come down the hall with a spatula in her hand.

"Okay, now. Do it again," she'd say. We'd sing it again. "Susie," Mama would interrupt, "you need to go up when Reba does so you don't sing the same note. And, Reba, you need to . . ." and so on until everything got settled. And before the potatoes burned on the stove, Mama got us in harmony.

A few months ago Mama called me and said, "You'll never guess what happened to us today."

I said, "What?"

She said, "Guess!"

I said, "Good Lord, Mama, we could be here all night!"

She laughed and said, "Well, a woman called here today wanting to talk to your daddy. So I walked down the hall and opened the bedroom door, where he was taking a nap."

By this time Daddy had gotten on the phone extension. "It made me so mad," he said, "I was sound asleep and she came banging in there and woke me up!"

"Who was it?" I asked.

"Well," said Mama, "you know that newspaper your daddy and me always get called *Cattleman's Weekly*? Well, they were having a sweepstakes where they were giving a brand-new Ford truck—"

Daddy interrupted, "And that lady called to tell me I won the truck!"

"You, hell!" Mama shouted. "You didn't enter the sweepstakes! I did! It's my truck!"

Daddy just giggled.

So, on November 6, Mama's birthday, they flew down to Alabama and claimed Mama's brand-new truck!

Daddy

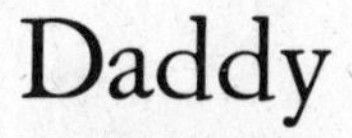

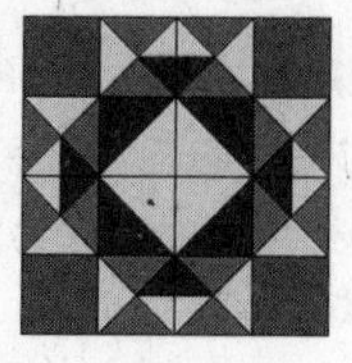

My father, Clark Vincent McEntire, was born on November 30, 1927. He was the only child of my grandparents John and Alice McEntire of Limestone Gap, Oklahoma.

Daddy shouldered a lot of responsibilities at a very early age. Grandpap and Uncle Keno, that was Grandpap's brother, treated Daddy like an equal, not as a son or a nephew. I always wondered why Daddy acted more mature than Grandpap. Maybe that was just the way Grandpap acted around us kids. We all worshiped him. But I later found out that Grandpap had acted that way all of his life. He was never very serious, always eager to pull a prank or act a little silly. He wasn't good at financial matters either. But to us kids he was IT! He'd give us a dime for a "sodie pop," or when we were down at the corral and had to walk up to the house for something, he'd tell us to hop in his "hoopie," which was his car, and drive up instead of walking. That made Daddy furious. For some reason, Daddy wanted us to get everything the hard way. He wanted better for us than he had growing up, but he didn't want us to get it too easily either.

Boy, can I relate to that!

In June 1997, Narvel and I took Mama and Daddy along with Alice's daughter, Garett, Brandon, Pake's daughter, Autumn, and Shelby on a three-week vacation to Europe. We had a wonderful time. But the best part was that we had a chance for all of us to really sit and talk, especially at dinnertime. That was something we didn't get to do much of back when we were growing up. Daddy called our dinner talk "chattering" and wanted it quiet while he ate his evening meal. Now, four kids and two adults at the supper table can get a little boring, especially for the kids, when eating is the only thing going on. We weren't used to that. Because when Daddy was off rodeoing or buying cattle and it was just Mama and us kids, we'd talk, cut up, tell jokes, and have a blast at the supper table. So when Daddy was home, we'd eat in silence until he was through and left the table. Then we could have our usual discussion about what had happened that day to each of us.

I felt for Daddy because he missed all the fun. He

missed all the stupid stuff us kids did for so many years. Stuff that we still laugh about and tell our kids when we all get together. Stuff that Daddy has no idea what we're talking about. That's sad. But on our vacation to Europe we had lots of time to sit and talk, listen and laugh. I learned a lot about my father on that trip.

For instance, Daddy told us that one night his mother was canning a side of beef and had run out of lids for her canning jars. So she sent Daddy up to the store about a mile away to buy some lids so she could complete her canning. Daddy walked to the store in the dark by himself. When he got back, Grandma told him that she needed more lids, that she had more beef than she thought, so he had to go back and buy some more. Daddy was only nine years old.

By the way, there weren't any streetlights, any sidewalks, and no pavement. It was only a dirt road, beaten out by a few car tires, wagon wheels, and horses' hooves, with the trees and bushes on each side. His only light would have been the moon up above. But there was the threat of snakes, wolves, panthers, and bears. Daddy walked by himself on a beat-out dirt road listening to every sound coming from the weeds and underbrush. He said on his second trip to the store he got to the railroad overpass and heard something squeal real loud! It could have been a tree owl or something bigger. He said every hair on his head stood up! But it didn't scare him nearly as bad as his mama would have if he didn't show back up with those lids!

I was pretty impressed, because when I was a teenager, I couldn't even muster up the courage to walk to our barn in the dark to let the horses out after they had eaten!

Life sure was different back then. Daddy also told us that Grandpap sent him on a train with two box-car loads of cattle from the cattle pens at the sub prison by Stringtown, Oklahoma (the railroad called it Flora), to Kansas City, Missouri, to sell them at the stockyards.

Daddy rode in the caboose with the conductor and the brakie (the brakeman). When they arrived at the rail yards in Kansas City, the train stopped. The train was broken, and thus left the caboose and other cars, except the cattle cars, which were usually put up at the front of the train.

Daddy started to get off the train, but the conductor told him to stay on, they would ride the coal car or engine to the stockyards. When they got there, Daddy found the commission man and he sold the cattle for Daddy. Daddy got his money and then rode the streetcar to Union Station. The railroad had given him a return ticket on the Katy passenger train, which he rode to McAlester, Oklahoma, and then caught the bus on home to Limestone Gap.

Daddy was thirteen years old.

I wouldn't dream of sending Shelby off by himself like that. He's only nine years old, I'm a very overprotective mother, and things are more dangerous and very different nowadays.

But my grandparents raised their son like they thought he should be raised, just like my parents raised us four kids like they thought it should be done. Now it's my responsibility to teach Shelby the morals and values of life that have been taught and passed down for the last three generations. But just like those past generations of McEntires, I'll do it like I think it should be done.

I think Daddy knows that. After all, I am his kid!

Sisters

Alice Lynn McEntire Stewart Beck Foran was born December 3, 1951, in McAlester, Oklahoma. She is the eldest, toughest, biggest-hearted protector of the McEntire kids!

Alice is my hero. She is a survivor. She has four children: the two oldest, Vince, happily married with three children, and Garett, an aspiring actress living in Los Angeles, are from her second husband, Brent Beck. Trevor, still in high school and dreaming of being a team roper or steer wrestler one day, and Haley, our little angel, still live at home with Alice and their dad, Robert.

When Haley was born, she was never expected to make it out of the hospital. Then they said she'd never live past her fifth birthday. She's thirteen years old now and loving life. She can't walk, can't talk, can't use the toilet, can't feed herself, but she has taught all of us that being perfect ain't all it's cracked up to be!

This child is still alive because of the never-ending, unconditional love she receives from her family and friends. She's a miracle baby. It hurts to see Alice look at physically normal kids. She has the saddest look on her face. When she feels me looking at her, she'll turn to me and say, "I'd give anything if Haley could do that." I've always heard that God never gives us more than we can handle. I know Alice has handled Haley's situation better than any of us other three would have. Thank God she has her husband, Robert. He's an angel with Haley, so are Trevor, Garett, Vince, and most of the town of Lane, Oklahoma!

Alice's nieces and nephews have always thought she hung the moon. She tells the best stories, she roughhouses with them just like she did her own kids, and anyone can see how much love she holds in her heart for children. I know Shelby and Chelsea love her. They can't wait to go see Aunt Alice.

One time we were out at the pool, talking, telling Wild West stories, and Alice started a story about her second husband, Brent Beck. Shelby and Chelsea were hanging on her every word.

She said, "One time, back when Brent was a little ol' boy about two years old, he started following a skunk around the front yard. The skunk was going back under the house, where evidently the rest of his family was. Brent reached out and got hold of the skunk's tail just before it disappeared from sight. The skunk, not liking this at all, sprayed Brent right in the face! He was blinded for almost four days!"

Chelsea looked over at Narvel and said, *"What was he thinking?!"*

When Alice was a couple of years old, she went out and sat on top of a huge red-ant bed! *What was she thinking?*

When Susie was little, she jumped out of the back of the pickup truck before it stopped. Not once, but twice! *What was she thinking?*

When Narvel was about seven or eight, he was out helping his dad mow the lot they owned. While Narvel Senior took his turn at mowing, my Narvel walked back to the car for a break. On his way to the car he found an old used cigarette butt lying on the ground. He picked it up, got into the car and pushed in the cigarette lighter and lit it up! Just about that time Narvel looked up and saw his dad walking back to the car. Narvel panicked and shut the lit cigarette up in the ashtray. His dad got in the car with him and smelled something burning. He pulled the ashtray open and said, "Now, how did that get in there?" Narvel said, "Boy, I don't know!" *What was he thinking?*

So I guess Alice isn't the only ornery person I know. I think I'm surrounded by them! But you know what? It sure does keep things interesting!

* * *

Martha Susan McEntire Luchsinger was born November 8, 1957. She is two years and eight months younger than I am. Susie is the only one of us kids born without red hair and freckles. We always said she was the most spoiled and pampered, and I guess that was so, especially since she was the baby of the family.

She was also the tightest one of the bunch when it came to money!

Daddy and Mama accumulated eight thousand acres of land when we were growing up. Daddy let us sell deer hunting permits for one dollar to anyone who wanted to hunt deer on our place. The money we made during deer hunting season was divided among us four kids and we used it to buy Christmas presents.

It was a well-known fact that Susie would still have some of her "deer hunting money" the next June.

Susie's daughter, Lucchese, spent a week with us here in Tennessee last November. She looks so much like Susie when she was that age. I got a big kick out of telling Lucchese my "Susie stories"!

Kimmie, our housekeeper and nanny, worked for Susie before she came to work for us. One day I said, "Kimmie, why don't we go up and take the clothes that Shelby has outgrown out of his closet?"

Kimmie looked over at me and said, "Is that a

'*Susie* we' or a '*we* we'?" I couldn't figure out what she was talking about, so she went on to explain. "Well, whenever Susie would want me to do something, she'd say, 'Why don't we . . .' and then she'd go off and do something else and leave me to do the chore. So that's why I was asking if it was a '*Susie* we' that I'd do alone or a '*we* we' and we'd do it together."

Susie was on the road with me for a while and she even worked in my office as my secretary. Since going off on her own several years ago, she has become a very popular country gospel singer who chose Christian country over country. She and her husband, Paul, travel all over the country singing and preaching the Gospel. They have three happy and healthy children, E.P., Lucchese, and Samuel Clark.

Last year I got inducted into the Oklahoma Heritage Hall of Fame in Tulsa, Oklahoma. Narvel, Cindy Owen, Starstruck's Vice President, Creative Services, and I left Nashville and flew via McAlester to pick up Mama, Daddy, Susie, and Nell Shaw, a friend of the family's. We got to Tulsa, got into the limousine, and drove over to the place where the ceremony was to be held.

I first took pictures, did interviews, and visited with the other five inductees. Then we were all taken into the ballroom for dinner. I was thrilled to see so many of my friends there. Ed and Natalie Gaylord, Red and Gail Steagall, Clem, Donna, and Bart

McSpadden, the whole bunch from the Texoma Medical Center, Jim and Sharon Shoulders, and Tom Carter, who helped me write my autobiography.

I was even happier that I sat by Susie during dinner. We had the best time that night. We laughed, we cut up, howled at each other's jokes, and basically enjoyed each other's company. That's how it should be between sisters! It's awful that we don't get to see each other more and that our kids don't get to spend more time together. I'm going to work on that. Alice, our big sister, would like that too!

I loved it because I got to thank Susie from the stage during my acceptance speech that she had cared enough to come with me to the ceremony.

When we flew back into McAlester and were saying our good-byes, I hugged Susie and told her, "Susie, if you ever need me, call me. I'll always be there for you."

And I know she would be there for me too if I ever called her.

Sisters are great!

A Big Brother

D*el Stanley McEntire was born June* 23, 1953, in McAlester, Oklahoma.

We called him Pake. When Mama was pregnant with Pake, Daddy would come in and pat Mama's stomach and say, "How's Pecos Pete doing today?" I wonder how Daddy knew it was going to be a boy. That was way before they could tell the sex of the baby by an ultrasound.

After Pake was born, Daddy named him Del Stanley, after Del Haverty, a bareback rider and bulldogger, and Stanley Gomez, another steer wrestler. But from so many fond references to the baby as Pecos Pete, the name Pake stayed. He's the only Pake I know. Pake is a year and nine months older than I am.

Pake and Katie, his wife, have three girls: Autumn, Calamity, and Chism.

My son, Shelby, is now nine years old. My granddaughter, Chelsea, is five. These two children are inseparable. They remind me of how it used to be between Pake and myself. They play together and fight together. I hope as they grow older the bond will stay as strong.

Pake's love in life has always been rodeoing. I think Pake was born thirty to one hundred years too late in life. He would have fit in just right in the time of *Lonesome Dove* or back when Grandpap was rodeoing.

This past August I was asked to speak at a motivational conference in Oklahoma City. Narvel, Sandi Spika, my stylist, Shelby, and I flew from Nashville to McAlester, Oklahoma, picked up Mama and Daddy, and then flew on to Oklahoma City. Pake, Calamity, Alice, Robert, Trevor, and Garett met us at the conference. Susie and her bunch were the only ones missing.

After the speech we all went down to the Cattleman's Steak House for lunch. That's one of Daddy's favorite places to eat in Oklahoma City. And since we all grew up on a working cattle ranch, beef is always on the table, ordered by at least one of us and sometimes more. We had a great visit, laughing, eating, telling jokes, saying how much each kid had grown, and catching up on what everyone had been doing. Pake left first; he was up that night at Ponca City, Oklahoma, at the rodeo. We said good-bye to Alice and her family and the rest of us flew back home.

Several days later I called Pake's house, needing to talk to Katie when, to my amazement, Pake answered the phone. The reason I was so shocked was because Pake had been gone almost all year long, selling insurance and rodeoing all over the country. He's hardly ever home with those two occupations. After "Hey Reberneller! What are you up to?"—my name is Reba Nell, but he finds it amusing to join the two together—his next words were "Hey, did you hear what I did at Ponca City?"

I said, "No, I haven't talked to anybody back home." He excitedly started telling me how Ace Bowman from Pawhuska, Oklahoma, tied the arena record in the first go-round of the 1998 Ponca City 101 Ranch Rodeo with a 9.7, which was previously set in 1993 by Buckey Heffner from Chelsea, Oklahoma.

Then it was Pake's turn to ride into the roping box. Pake nodded his head, the roping chute was opened, the steer came out, and Pake and his horse were after the steer in hot pursuit! Pake tied his steer down in 9.0 seconds flat!!!! He had broken the arena record!!

Pake said that a bunch of the cowboys that he'd rodeoed with all his life were there that night. They all came over and congratulated him, gave him high-fives and low-fives, hit him on the back and shared in what Pake called the most exciting nine seconds of his life. I guess my motivational speech in Oklahoma City worked!

Pake was born left-handed. But that was before he broke his left arm in two places at Uncle Slim's arena in Stringtown, Oklahoma. He was riding a calf that our cousin Doris Jean put him on. They had been out at the arena all day having fun, and Doris Jean told him this would be the last calf to ride since it was so hot and they needed to go to the house and get cleaned up. He rode the calf, but when he jumped off he landed on his left arm and broke it. They took him to the hospital.

Mama begged the doctors to let her wash his arm, but they said no. Eight weeks later, when the cast came off, big sores had developed, and the dirt and grime were still there. It was a wonder he didn't lose it! Boy, Mama was so mad! Not because he broke his arm, but because they didn't wash his arm off before they put the cast on it!

This was only weeks before starting the first grade. Mrs. Kelly, who taught all four of us kids in first grade, started him out writing right-handed because of his cast. That was always a conversation piece. Pake would write right-handed but he would rope left-handed. That in itself is a big handicap, because most all arenas are built for right-handed ropers. So in 1989 Pake got up the courage to change over to roping right-handed. It took him a while, but it paid off big-time!

But that wasn't Pake's only handicap. Pake was constantly under the pressure of being the son and grandson of Clark and John McEntire, two world champion cowboys. He's always wanted so badly to follow in their footsteps and win the world. That's a lot of pressure for a young man. I've always thought about that situation, having a son of my own. I've never encouraged Shelby or discouraged him about following in my footsteps. I have told him several times that I would help him prepare a song to sing for the school Christmas program if he wanted to sing. He'd say, "No, that's okay, Mom. I don't want to." Then he'd wait a little while and ask, "Mom, did I hurt your feelings that I said I didn't want to sing a song?" I said, "No, honey, it didn't hurt my feelings. I just want you to know I'll be there to help you if you ever want to sing."

Right now Shelby has no interest in the music business. Either way is fine with me. I only want him to be happy. He told me he wants to either play ice hockey, be a bull rider, or be a jet pilot. What's a mother to do?!

I understood how much Pake craved, needed, loved, and wanted this win, this accomplishment. I could appreciate it more than most people, because I rodeoed with Pake for several years. I was there when there were more "no paychecks" than paychecks! But I was also with Pake when he won the Post, Texas, Steer Roping back in 1972. They presented him with a hand-tooled leather saddle and a silver trophy. We were thrilled to death. Daddy had won the same roping in 1971, and Pake won it again in 1974. Second generation carrying on the tradition. Speaking of "carrying on the tradition," in the early 1930s Grandpap rode his horse and led another one to the 101 Ranch Rodeo in Ponca City from Stonewall, Oklahoma, approximately 180 miles one way. Daddy said he missed his steer, rode out of the back end of the arena, got his lead horse, and headed home.

I remember all the years down in the roping pen, when Pake talked us girls into helping him by putting the steers into the roping chute and turning them out while he sat up on his horse and got ready to rope them. We had the dirty end of the fun! Those steers kicked us, stepped on our feet, pushed us into the fence, but for some reason we said yes to Pake. We were always there for each other.

It's great having a brother and sisters. It meant having someone to play with, to argue with, to fight with, but always to take up for and for them to take up for you. I moved to Nashville in 1987. All the rest of my family are still in Oklahoma. We don't see each other as much as we used to, but we sure burn up the telephone wires!

Not long ago Pake and Katie came to Nashville to see Autumn, their eldest daughter, who is attending Belmont University here in Nashville. Pake called me one morning and said, "Reberneller! This is Pake. I'm in jail in Albuquerque! I need you to come bail me out!"

I said, "I'll be right there!" He laughed his same old familiar laugh that sounds more and more like Daddy's and Grandpap's, and told me they were on their way out to our house. As usual, I couldn't wait to see him.

And by the way . . . I would have gone to Albuquerque.

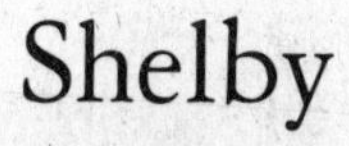

Shelby

Mama always said, "Reba, you've never lived until you've had a child of your own." She was right, of course. Since we had Shelby, every day is Mother's Day!

For years I didn't want to be a parent. I didn't want to be a mother. I thought that my career was going great and I didn't want to make time to start a family. But in 1989, when Narvel and I decided to have a child, that decision changed my life.

Shelby Steven McEntire Blackstock was born February 23, 1990, in Nashville, Tennessee, at 5:04 in the morning.

Shelby is the greatest thing that has ever happened to me! He is the absolute highlight of my life.

He is my sunshine, he is the funniest thing. Shelby brings out the kid in me. He makes me silly, he makes me goofy, I get to do things with him that I probably am not supposed to do now that I'm a grown-up, but he reminds me of how I still like to do them.

Shelby is what unconditional love is all about! But, of course, every mother knows that! The love that a child receives from a mama means that no matter what they do, you still love them. You might bust their butt, but you still love them.

Shelby is full of energy and always wanting my attention. I'm glad he wants it. It would crush me if he didn't!

It's a very familiar sound when no matter what I'm doing I hear "Hey, Mom, come here!"

And that little voice doesn't really care where we are either. I heard it several times in Hawaii, where we took a family vacation. We had a wonderful time. It's such a beautiful place to visit, I wouldn't even mind living there someday. When I sit at the pool at the Princeville Sheraton Hotel on the island of Kauai and look toward the ocean, it's the most spiritual view on earth. I love to get up early and walk down on the beach. The tide is out, so you can walk way out on the ocean floor and see what it looks like without the water on top.

One evening we had reservations for a luau down by the pool. We read the hotel's directions that said we were to check in at the bar. Shelby looked over at

Chelsea and said, "All right, Chelsea! We get to go into the bar!" I looked down at him and said, "What would you do if you went inside?" He answered, "I'd order me a piña colada with rocks on top and no salt!" I have a feeling he meant a margarita on the rocks with no salt, but who knows, it might be a good-tasting drink!

That's kind of like the time he was in kindergarten and the class went on a field trip to a Mexican restaurant near the school. When I went to pick up Shelby from school that day, his teacher, Mrs. Rivera, said, "Shelby sure does like Mexican food! He knew just what to order." I instantly became a little suspicious and asked what he did actually order.

She said, "He ordered a burrito and to drink he wanted a frozen strawberry daiquiri made by virgins!"

I just hope he doesn't want to be a bartender when he grows up.

When he was three years old, we were at a hotel in Florida and he told me that he wanted to be a bellman when he grew up. I asked him why, and he said, "So I can always push the buttons on the elevator."

One day we were driving somewhere and Shelby from the backseat said, "Dad, when are we going to be there?"

Narvel said, "In just a little while. How come?"

Shelby replied, "'Cause, Dad, I'm getting *bull*

sick!" I have no idea why he called "car sick" "bull sick"! For a time he called it "barn sick."

Parenting is a very humbling experience but never more so than when you find yourself caught up in your kids' homework. I thought second-grade math and spelling were going to send Narvel and me around the bend, but now Shelby is in the third grade and it's not getting any easier for us. Shelby's doing fine, but I don't know if Narvel and I can hang in there! It's so much more advanced now than when we were kids.

Things are quite different in the third grade compared to the first two. The teachers urge the children to take on more responsibility, and that helps them mature.

After fifteen minutes of visiting and going over Shelby's strong and weak points in his classes, one of his six teachers told me that Shelby one day called her "little missy"! She said, "I've never been called that before!"

One of Shelby's papers in language arts class made it to the school newspaper. In our parent-teacher meeting, Shelby's "little missy" teacher found out from me that the story wasn't true, that Shelby had made the whole story up, basing it on an event in the life of his older brother, Brandon. She was totally shocked. All the other teachers started laughing. She looked at them, puzzled, and they told her they all knew it wasn't true. Shelby had told them not to tell "little missy."

We faxed it to Grandma Jac, and she replied, "Shelby, I would have given you an A+!! Very good! Love, Grandma Jac."

That really made Shelby feel good!

Of course, school is not just for learning, book learning, that is. Narvel and I were in Florida for four days of shows. I called home to ask Shelby how his first day of school went. He said, "Mama, Bobby told everyone in school today that I'm in love with Lynette!"

I asked him what Lynette said about it, and he told me she said, "Well, did you have to tell everyone in school?"

He told his dad that he liked Lynette because last year she had hit him on the playground and she was tough.

Kimmie and Shelby were taking me to the airport, so I could go to one of my shows. Kimmie and I were talking about cleaning out the freezer at the house because we were thinking about butchering one of the eighty steers Brandon was feeding, packaging it up, and putting it in the freezer.

I looked over my shoulder at Shelby and jokingly said to Kimmie, "Don't tell Brandon."

Well, this really upset Shelby. Brandon will never find another person in the world who would take up for him like Shelby.

He quickly said, "I'm gonna tell Brandon!"

I said, "No, you're not."

He said, "Mom, we've been so nice to those steers and if we kill one of them, they'll think we hate them!"

I said, "Shelby, it'll be okay. Look at it this way, we'll be able to have steaks, hamburger meat, roasts, and T-bones for supper! It'll be great!"

He thought about it a moment and said, "Can't we just eat out?"

Shelby, Brandon, and Kimmie were over near the barn, looking at the hay that had just been cut and would soon be put into bales. Brandon was driving the Gator, which is like a small tractor, through the pasture, getting out, and kicking the cut grass around, when Shelby said, "Brandon, this is not good."

Brandon said, "What do you mean, Shelby?"

Shelby replied, "You're not doing the hay any good."

"Why?" asked Brandon.

Shelby said, "Brandon, you don't have any idea where those tires have been!"

When Narvel and I were off on a business trip, we called home one afternoon. Shelby got on the phone and wasn't very happy. Narvel said, "Shelby, what's wrong?"

Shelby went on to tell his dad how the older kids were bossing him around and being mean to him. Narvel asked what he could do to make it better. Shelby said, "I don't know, Dad. I just wish I had a better family."

A few weeks before one of our family vacations, Kimmie had brought Shelby back three hermit crabs from New Jersey, after visiting her family up there. That was a new and different addition to our family that I wasn't really for at the beginning. But Kimmie and Shelby won and the hermit crabs settled into our home. At least they stayed in a covered aquarium!

While we were in Hawaii, Shelby, Shawna, Harley, Chelsea, Melissa, Brandon's fiancée, Brandon, and Chassidy were all down at the pool, swimming. Harley was saying how he was a little homesick and was ready to get back home and see his daddy and brother. Shelby said he missed Bandit, his dog, really bad too. Melissa said, "I didn't know you had a dog," joking with Shelby.

Shelby defending himself said rather loudly, "Yes, I do! I have a dog! And I have crabs too!"

You should have seen the heads turn.

We started renovating our house in December of 1996. In January of 1997 it became impossible to stay in the house while the workers were there. So we leased a house close to Hermitage, Tennessee, and moved the whole family over there. Everyone except Shawna and Chelsea. They stayed in the apartment over the barn at the house.

Because Brandon had to go to the barn every morning to work, he had the job of taking Shelby to school. Brandon would even get Shelby up in the morning, oversee him getting dressed, feed him his breakfast, and off they would go!

Brandon found out that Shelby was waking up on his own before the alarm went off and lying in bed, watching TV. So he told Shelby that when he woke up, go ahead and get dressed. That would save time and Brandon wouldn't have to oversee Shelby getting dressed.

So one night Brandon woke up and had to go to the bathroom. He went through Shelby's bedroom because it was on the way and because he saw that Shelby's light was on. When he walked into Shelby's bedroom, he saw Shelby lying at the foot of his bed, fully clothed and sound asleep.

Brandon looked over at the clock, it was 4:05 A.M.! Does that kid mind or what?!

Brandon woke Shelby up and got him back in bed. Later that morning he asked Shelby why he was lying at the foot of his bed with all his clothes on.

Shelby said, "Well, I woke up and thought it was time to go to school, so I got dressed. I fell asleep waiting on you to come get me!"

That's why I fly home after every concert I can. I don't know what fresh story or new adventure of his I am missing firsthand.

Don't You Hate It When Women Are Right?

S*helby is so proud that sometimes* he gets frustrated when I try to help him with his homework. He wants me to believe that he knows it all already. When he was learning how to tell time, he and I disagreed about whether the answer to his homework problem was ten minutes till or ten minutes after.

I said, "Put down my answer, and I'll write a note to your teacher telling her that if it's wrong to give me the failing grade, not you."

Shelby said, "Okay, but I just know you got it wrong, Mama!"

The next day he came home from school and I said, "Shelby, who was right?"

He hung his head and said, "You were."

I said, "You hate it when a woman is right, don't you, son?"

"Yes, ma'am."

"Well," I said, "get used to it!"

A Sentimental Mother Is an Interior Decorator's Biggest Nightmare

My husband, Narvel, has great taste! And I'm not just talking about in women! He and I are as different as day and night in many areas, one being our taste in interior decorating. He goes for the right size, colors that blend and match the rest of the room and go with the color palette of the house, style, era, etc.

When Narvel was growing up in Burleson, Texas, he always dreamed of living in a brick house. All the houses in the better part of Fort Worth, Texas, were brick. Narvel and his parents lived in a wood-frame house. When he was sixteen years old, Narvel got married. That same year his mother and father moved into a beautiful "brick" home. It's not that Narvel was around fancy things all his life, it's just that he always wanted them! Nicer things. He's watched and he's learned throughout the years and has picked up new ideas wherever we go.

I, on the other hand, grew up a little farther north than Narvel, in Chockie, Oklahoma. Population eighteen! I was never worried or concerned about fashion, what matched, what didn't, never looked at magazines to see what the latest fashions were or even cared, for that matter! All of my clothes were hand-me-downs. Passed down from either our cousins or Alice. It didn't matter if the clothes were too big; to me they were new and something different to wear. The only thing I ever wanted in the way of fashion was a shiny new outfit to wear when I was running barrels at the rodeo. I loved going to the National Finals Rodeo in Oklahoma City. My favorite event to watch, of course, was the ladies' barrel-racing event. That's because that was the event I competed in. I never made the top fifteen contestants at the National Finals Rodeo, but I always dreamed of it. The ladies would wear beautiful, colorful, shiny pants and tops to match, sometimes even have a rhinestone hatband to top off their outfit. I guess I was preparing myself just in case I ever made it to the top!

My girlfriends were a lot more fashion conscious than I was. But that still wasn't saying much. In Kiowa, Oklahoma, I don't remember anyone setting any trends. And me, I was too much of a tomboy to even care. But I came about this honestly. I got it from my mama. I'm just like my mother. I never knew her being too concerned about what we kids wore just as long as it was clean. To preserve our school clothes, after we got home she would make us change into something that was older and not as nice.

Now, Narvel and I have traveled quite extensively together over the past eighteen years and even more recently have gotten to visit museums, palaces, and great estates in North America, Europe, and Australia. I also have the ability and finances to seek the input of fancy interior decorators for our home. That overcomes 98 percent of my having no taste in interior decorating!

But Mama never had that luxury. We did have a few nice things passed down from Daddy's mother. Things like fine crystal, real silverware, and fine linens. But those things were either kept in the china closet or in the trunk. We didn't take them into everyday use. And the only museum I ever remember us going to was in Cody, Wyoming, when I was in the first grade. While we were going from one rodeo to the next, we stopped at the western art museum there and went through it. I'll never forget it.

Mama's style of interior decorating was a lot more in the "sentimental mode"! I remember going into Mama's bedroom when I was a kid. She loves to read! Everywhere you looked, there would be books and magazines! But the thing I remember the best is that she would prop up against her dresser mirror the latest drawing or card that one of us kids had made for her. Again, I take after my mama! I go with whatever Shelby has made and brought home from school or a Cub Scout meeting! I have more creative artwork made out of aluminum pie pans, twine, nuts and bolts, plastic soda bottles, paper plates, yarn, wood, and candles! Who could pass that up? I catch Shelby walking into my bathroom and making sure that his Cub Scout projects are still in their same place on my vanity.

That reminds me of another time when Shelby came home with his T-ball trophy. He'd played T-ball that past summer and had a great time with all the other kids his age. Everyone who played received a gold trophy. We were having a small dinner party that night, and Shelby stated that he'd put the trophy right in the center of the table, so everyone could see it. He was sharing his prized possession with us. I was telling Shelley Browning, who runs Starstruck Films for me and who is the mother of five children, this story. She thought it was so sweet that Shelby was showing my friends that he, too, could win a trophy, just like his mom. So the next day I walked Shelby downstairs to where I keep the trophies that I have won and I said, "Shelby, this isn't my trophy case, it belongs to the whole family. So you can put your trophy in here, anywhere you want."

He said, "Really, Mom?!" He was so excited. He held his trophy and walked back and forth until he found just the right spot. It was on the middle shelf, dead center, and eye level for Shelby. That's where it's stayed ever since.

Narvel's fantasy was to have a home that looked like a picture from one of those architectural magazines—perfect! Although I've never seen the "sentimental mode" in any of those magazines, it's definitely my favorite style!

A Bone to Pick

We*'ve all used that expression "I've* got a bone to pick with you." Somewhere along the way I learned an old folk saying that always seemed to me to be an interesting variation on that expression, but one which I think packs a lot of truth. If you want to succeed in life, the saying goes, you must pick three bones to carry with you at all times: a wishbone, a backbone, and a funnybone.

Those are three "bones" I always carry with me.

My wishes and dreams have always driven me forward over the biggest bumps and deepest potholes.

My stubborn, "no-quit" philosophy keeps my nerve strong at all times.

And, perhaps, most important of all, I make sure

to keep a sense of humor and perspective about things, and I try to make sure laughter fills every day.

With those three building bones, I believe you have your best chance of always standing tall and going far.

Rodeo Time

I *just don't have the time to* do everything I have to do. There always seems to be too much to do at the end of each day for most of us. On the one hand, perhaps that shows that we're full of ambitious plans, but it sure gets frustrating to feel that no matter how much you accomplish, you feel like you're moving at half-speed while the world and time go whizzing by your head at some kind of speed that you see only in movies like *Star Wars.*

When time pressures threaten to totally stress me out, I do have one little trick I try that usually makes me feel a whole lot better. If I'm having one of those days when it just seems like there are seventy-two hours of work to be squeezed into my twenty-four-hour day, I think back to my good ol' rodeo days.

The summer months were the busiest times for

rodeoing, but it became especially busy on the Fourth of July weekend! That's when a serious cowboy or cowgirl could enter and make three rodeos in one day. The towns were Livingston, Montana; Red Lodge, Montana; and Cody, Wyoming. It was tough, but if you drew up right, you could do it. I've done it and so have hundreds of others in the rodeo business.

That's what you call time management. Cramming as much as possible into one day.

I've seen Pake and our cousin, Don Wayne Smith, rope their calves during the slack that morning; leave their horses, trucks, and trailer; catch a plane; get to another town, where they were also entered; borrow a horse; and rope their calves at that rodeo that same night.

I don't think it was nearly as competitive in Daddy's and Grandpap's day of rodeoing. But Daddy had to manage taking care of eight thousand acres and more than three thousand head of steer and then find the time to still make it to a steer roping.

Let's take my rodeo event, which was barrel racing. Your goal is to get on your horse and maneuver your way around each of three barrels, which are laid out on the arena floor in a triangle. You have to ride around the barrels in a cloverleaf pattern, and whoever rides around the barrels the fastest without knocking one over (which gets you a five-second penalty) wins.

Now, also bear in mind that the animal you're trying to get to run around those barrels is maybe fifteen to sixteen hundred pounds of thundering horseflesh that you want to break out of the gate like a bat out of hell. Then you want him to stop just as fast as you turn around that first barrel, then repeat it twice more—all in a matter of seconds. And the trick, of course, is not just to get it done faster than any of the other racers but to come out of there still on the horse and with your hide in one piece. It's very high-speed and it can be dangerous. I've seen horses fall down and roll over on girls and I've seen the horse stop to turn, causing the rider to run her head into a wall.

Yes, barrel racing forces you to shut out all other distractions, to focus on this great (kind of crazy) challenge, and to pack into a very few seconds a whole flood of activities. Everything goes by in a blur, so you never do think about it and stop to appreciate how much you can get done in a few seconds until it's all over. Of course, it takes many hours of training for the horse and rider to accomplish this with victory.

Now, try thinking about, say, a steer roper who's not only got to control his horse but has to try to throw his rope around the horn of one huge steer that does not want to get caught and is not shy about his feelings. A steer roper is somebody who can juggle a few tasks simultaneously that usually makes whatever tasks you're trying to juggle seem just a little less challenging. Or picture a bronc rider who blasts out of the gate barely seated on top of some of the biggest, nastiest creatures who ever bucked on four feet. Those bronc riders are just hoping to hang on for eight seconds without getting thrown and stomped on. *Eight seconds!*

I guess time management has been very key to the McEntire family for several generations. It has allowed me the training I need today to juggle working on an album, writing a book, developing a movie project, and touring all over the world, all at the same time. All these projects have time schedules that are very important to their success. It seems the clock has been ticking all of my life.

Water from the Well

It's *challenging for me to raise* a child in the lifestyle we have today when I still want him to know the hardships and hard times my parents and grandparents had and the no-frills way I was brought up. I want Shelby to have nicer things and to experience all the fun and exciting events of life, but I have to make sure he appreciates them and never takes them for granted. That's hard to do when I get caught up in our lifestyle as well.

I've never had it so good, and you always want to share the good things with the ones you love.

But thankfully, we've got my daddy as a living salute to what was good about the good ol' days.

One night we were all in Florence, Italy, eating supper in a renovated fifteenth-century monastery where we were staying. While we were waiting for our entrees, Daddy started counting the glasses on the table. I noticed it first and then Garett, my niece, did as well. She said, "Grandpa, what are you doing?"

He said, "Twenty-seven glasses on the table! Kids, I never saw glasses on the dinner table until I started dating your ma and was over at her house having Sunday dinner." Of course this struck all of us as unusual.

"What did y'all do when you needed a drink during your meal?" I asked.

"You got up," he stated matter-of-factly, "and went over to the water bucket and picked up the dipper and got a drink out of it, just like everyone else did."

Now, Mama said that when she was very small, they had only one fork and Grandpa got to use that. Everyone else ate with spoons. When Grandma Reba and Grandpa Elvin got married in 1922, they went to the dump and picked up dishes, cracked usually, and cooking utensils that were all bent, but evidently people just didn't throw away forks.

One thing we learned during our European vacation was that bread in Europe is very hard! Daddy had a rough time with that. Every night Narvel would order a bottle of wine and Daddy would have a glass or two with dinner. With the bread being too hard to bite into, Daddy would dip his bread in his wine to soften it up. That sure got some strange looks from the wine stewards!

Daddy said, "I'd give anything for a good ol' buttermilk biscuit!"

Daddy got pretty homesick during that vacation. We thought he was going to jump ship on us several times. He said, "Back home our county seat ain't seven miles from the house. If I ever get home, I doubt I'll ever see it again. I'm not even gonna go down to the mailbox!"

Yes, you can take the man out of the country, but you can't take the country out of the man!

Tougher than You Think

J*ust about the only fear I* have these days is the one everyone else has—getting sick. I don't think about it, because I believe that if you think about getting sick, you will get sick. You'll worry about it, stress out about it, and that's the main thing that gets you in that situation.

I've learned during all my years of living that your mind is tougher than you think! And if you let your mind focus on what you need your body to do, you can get through your daily challenges with some pretty powerful help. You can talk to your body and thank it for getting you through the day. Thank it for doing such a great job of avoiding the colds and flus. This causes a positive attitude for you, your mind, and your body. It sure works for me.

God gave me this body. And I try to take care of it

the best I know how. I wasn't always this in tune with my body, and I regret how I abused it while I was growing up.

I lay out in the sun for too long a time without any sunscreen on. Now I don't even go outside without sunscreen on.

I overdid it on the alcohol when I was in college, and now I've learned to drink moderately and only socially.

I lifted thirty- and fifty-pound sacks of cattle feed every other day working my way through college. I lifted them incorrectly. I didn't know any better. I do now. But thank goodness I don't have to tote feed to cattle anymore!

I never was a water drinker. Now you'll never see me without a bottle of water. I'm a "waterholic"!

When we were growing up, fried food was a part of every meal we ate. Daddy would fry up the bacon, fry the eggs in the bacon grease, and then make the milk gravy out of the grease, milk, and flour. We'd even have fried bologna sandwiches for lunch. Nowadays the fried foods are few and far between.

I think dealing with fear is something each of us has to face in our own way. Since adulthood, I've never been afraid of dying. My faith gets credit for that. I fear for my loved ones getting hurt more than I fear for myself. But I've learned to put them in God's hands. It always goes back to "Thy kingdom come. Thy will be done." That means that I pray for God's will in all of our lives. He knows best and has the greatest plan for our lives.

Fear is the unknown. Fear is what we are not accustomed to. Face it head-on and it usually turns out to be much smaller and not nearly as threatening as you thought. Bring it out in the light. Fear is dark, truth is the light.

But I'm still afraid of snakes! And I darn sure don't want to go face-to-face with one of them! So I guess there are exceptions!

Grass Roots

Narvel *is what we call in* the Blackstock house a "treeaholic"! He loves to go walking down the drive in front of our house and to look up at our trees to see how all of them are doing.

Me, I come from a long line of folks who cleared out the trees and the brush so the grass could grow. But I still love trees, the bigger the better. That's definitely one of the things Narvel and I have in common, though he is just a little more attentive to trees than I am.

Now, when it comes to roots, the real growing kind, mine are grass. It seems like Daddy and Mama have spent their whole life trying to get grass to grow on our rocky hills in southeastern Oklahoma. They've done a great job of it.

As a kid, I remember Daddy hiring bulldozers to

come in and push the trees down and shove the brush into piles so he could burn them. All for the grass to grow. When the grass would grow, the cattle could then be put into the pastures to eat the grass. The more grass the cattle would eat, the fatter they would get; the fatter they would get, the more they would weigh when we sold them. The more they would weigh, the more money we could make! Grass was important.

At our house in Nashville we have a thirty-acre lawn. Brandon and the guys have seeded the lawn with rye grass. It's beautiful and green, especially in the winter, when everything else has died and turned brown. I can't tell you how many times Daddy has suggested that we turn some of our steers out onto the lawn so they could eat the grass instead of our having to mow it. Daddy can't quite comprehend the concept of a decorative lawn. To him, grass is a means of survival, not something pretty to look at.

The Best Seat of All

It seems like all my life I've been traveling. First of all, I was on the road with the whole family when Daddy was rodeoing. We took off from Chockie, Oklahoma, Mama and Daddy in the front seat and all four of us kids in the back, in a light green four-door Ford that had no air conditioner or radio.

As you can imagine, this was not smooth, quiet, comfortable transportation, but we loved those trips because we were all together. Maybe a little *too* together. With the four kids in the backseat, there was usually a lot of wrestling and fighting. When we traveled at night Susie and I—Mama called us "the little girls"—would get on the floor on either side of the hump, and there was no carpet in those days, just rough plastic sheeting on the floorboards. Alice got the actual seat, and Pake perched up above the seat.

Of course, there were no interstates back then, so Daddy would take us through the little towns with the two-horse trailer behind us. There were no automatic brakes like you have on the fancy trailers now. Daddy would see a red light up ahead and step on the brakes, which would send Pake flying down on top of Alice, knocking them both down onto Susie and me, and we'd have another big ol' "get-off-of-me" wrestling match. And we "little girls" aimed to give back as good as we got. By the time we got all sorted out and back in place, chances are here would come another town and another red light.

Pro wrestling's loss became music's gain, though, because it was on these long car trips that Mama taught us kids how to sing. We'd go down the road singing our little hearts out. That entertained us for many miles. And little did we know that it would prepare us for our future careers. It got us ready for the singing part as well as the traveling part.

My next stage of traveling came when Mama would cart us kids to singing gigs, to rodeos where we were competing, or to one of our basketball games. We'd moved way up in our mode of transportation by this time. The car had a radio and an air conditioner, but we continued to sing and wrestle anywhere we went.

Then, when I got into college, I started traveling with other barrel racers or with Pake to rodeos. Pake had a pickup and a camper with a horse trailer that was a lot nicer than anything we'd had before.

But the real traveling came after I received my recording contract in 1976. That's when I got a taste of the classier side of being on the road!

Since Red Steagall discovered me, I guess he felt responsible to teach me as much as possible. So I got to go on several road trips with Red Steagall and the Coleman County Cowboys in Red's big Silver Eagle bus! That was a blast! I'd never seen anything like that before! We'd play fairs in Shreveport, Louisiana; Lewistown, Montana; Casper, Wyoming; and even did a show in New Orleans, Louisiana. I'd open the show for Red, then I'd run around to the back bleachers, find a seat, and watch his entire show. I loved to hear him sing, but more than that I loved his jokes and stories. Red is the best storyteller and poet I've ever heard.

It was always fun getting to open the show for Red. I would be the only girl on the bus and I'd have a blast listening to all their road stories and things that had happened to them onstage with Red. I always had the best seat on the bus.

In 1978 I got my first band. I didn't make nearly enough money to travel in the big fancy Silver Eagles, so we went in cars and pickup trucks. Then we graduated to a modified van that leaked when it rained, with a horse trailer behind it in which we carried all of our equipment. It sure wasn't very nice to look at, but we got there! Later on we purchased a van and trailer that matched and didn't leak. We thought we were sitting in high cotton! There were five band members who rode in the van and took turns driving. There wasn't room for Susie and me, so we traveled in a car and took turns driving.

In May of 1982 I finally bought my first bus. I called it my Mother's Day present. I didn't have any kids, but I guess I acted like a mother to my band and sometimes they sure acted like a bunch of kids! So I guess that sort of made me a road mother. We had a lot of great times together.

It didn't matter what sort of transportation I was traveling in. The most important thing to me was that I arrived in time to sing and fulfill my commitment. Mama and Daddy had always taught us kids: If you say you're going to do something, then, by golly, you'd better be there and do it and do it to the best of your ability!

One year they had booked me at an afternoon concert in a park. The only problem was, the booking agent failed to calculate how many miles we had to travel from the show the night before to that next show and that we had to cross a time change. We lost an hour.

We pulled up to the venue just about the time we were to go onstage. We were already dressed and ready to play, but we still had to set up all the equipment and check it. There probably weren't one hundred people in the audience, but thank God they sat there patiently while we got ready.

One year, back when I was opening the show for George Strait and Conway Twitty, I had to fly in early to the town where we were performing to go to the radio station and do some interviews. The band was coming in on the bus, but it broke down a couple of hundred miles out. They rented a school bus and got all their equipment out and came on just in time to play the show. When they pulled up I asked them, "What did you get from the bus for me to wear?" They looked at each other, hoping someone had thought about that. No one had. So I went onstage that night wearing exactly what I had worn from home and to do the interviews in. *The show must go on!*

Then in 1989, when I was five months pregnant with Shelby, I told Narvel we should probably cancel the last two weekends. The roads were very rough and I thought that being on the bus so much would hurt the baby. But being the professional manager he is, Narvel leased a Learjet for the last two weeks of my tour. We loved it so much, we've been flying ever since.

Traveling to Europe was always very scary to me until we just jumped in with both feet and started going over the Atlantic Ocean and checking it out.

Our first few trips over were on a commercial airline and took eight to ten hours of flying time. Then we heard about this plane called the Concorde that flies from New York to London in three hours and fifteen minutes. We were hooked! And along with the borders being open in Europe, it felt a lot friendlier to us. On one of our trips over to Ireland, we got the opportunity to go to Cobh, a port near Cork in the southeastern part of Ireland. That is where the emigrants got on the boats going to the United States or to Australia. We learned that because of the potato famine in Ireland during the late 1860s, many people left. Most of the time they could afford to send only one family member away. They would have a wake, just as if the family member were dead. They knew they would never see them again.

The trip from Ireland to Ellis Island would take weeks and weeks. Narvel and I saluted their bravery, their courage, and their stamina. They made us appreciate all the more that we had the best seat in the house traveling on the Concorde.

Still, when it comes to travel, I find I get my greatest pleasure from returning to my earliest and simplest means of getting where I'm going.

It's a lot of fun to be with family! They laugh with you when you're silly, they get to you when you're out of line, they correct you when you don't tell a joke just right, and they are a blast to sing with. Back when I was a kid, it was my brother, sisters, and mama. Now it's with my three stepkids, my son-in-law, my granddaughter, my son, and husband. You should hear us sometime—well, maybe not, but it's sure interesting.

Especially at Christmastime! We'll head off in the Suburban, all of us quiet as mice, and Narvel will break into "Jingle Bells"! Everybody immediately joins in! But the most adventurous song we perform is our rendition of "The Twelve Days of Christmas"! One day we need to record that! Well, maybe not.

We get into the song, and on about the third day of Christmas we forget what comes next and we are making up our own things "my true love gave to me." The sixth day is "a six-pack of beer," nine is "nine people going into town to eat Mexican food," five is "five golf balls," and it gets worse from there on out!

So really, I have gone full circle when it comes to my transportation. Because once again I'm in a car full of the people I love dearly. Just like in the good old days!

The one thing I've learned is, no matter what the type of transportation, no matter what the destination, the best seat is always next to the people you love. That always makes for a great trip.

On Ice

O*ne of the most exciting aspects* to being a mom is the way your child will get you involved in all kinds of new things that you never expected to find yourself caught up in.

Some of those things like Power Rangers or video games just didn't exist when I was a kid. Probably computers are the most amazing development that Shelby and I are sharing these days. It's all-new and ever-changing and we love it. If I keep at it, I can maybe stay half a jump ahead of him on the learning curve, but soon he'll leap right past me, I know.

I love my computers, I take my laptop with me wherever I go so I can e-mail everyone literally around the world. Our fan club now communicates regularly by e-mail, which allows me to write more regularly than our printed newsletter did, and I sent frequent *e-postcards* to all my fans from the different countries of our recent European tour. And I've written this entire book on my laptop, usually backstage or flying to and from my concerts! Years ago I never would have imagined writing a book, let alone writing one on a computer that's smaller and lighter than my makeup bag!

But equally amazing to me are the common everyday objects that you get a whole new appreciation for when seen through your child's eyes.

Take ice, for example.

All the years I lived at home in Chockie, Oklahoma, we worked and lived on eight thousand acres of rocky, brushy poor country, as Daddy called it. When we were growing up, Daddy was gone a lot of the time rodeoing. That left Mama to stay at home and take care of the livestock and us kids. Believe me, she had her hands full.

A very vivid memory for me was all of us kids and Mama going down to the pond right below the hay barn during the winter months. Us kids went with Mama mainly to get to skate on the ice. We didn't have store-bought skates, or any other kind for that matter. We skated with our boots or shoes on. Mama, on the other hand, would take the big chopping ax down to the pond and break the ice so the animals would have water to drink.

One morning while we were at the pond, Mama was busy doing her thing while all of us kids were having the time of our life! It's funny that I can still hear the start of the cracking of the ice; the way it sounded was almost like the noise sonic waves make in those submarine movies. I also remember looking up while I was skating there at the edge of the pond. I was always too afraid to get very far from the edge. Oh, but not Susie! I looked up when Pake yelled at her to get back over where we were! There she was, right in the middle of the pond.

Now, it wasn't that big of a pond and Mama told me later that it wasn't over six feet deep, but at the time I thought my little sister was going to disappear from the face of the earth.

Mama calmly talked her back over to the edge where we were, and everything was okay. I've never been all that thrilled about being out on the ice since then.

In another part of the world, far away from us, there was a sport becoming very popular called ice hockey. It wasn't exactly on the radar screen in Chockie, Oklahoma, so consequently, we knew very little about it.

Little did I know that years later that sport would

become part of my world. My little boy, Shelby, loves to play hockey. He started at the age of seven and loves his time on the ice. And, of course, there's his mom with his dad up in the stands, now thinking that being on the ice is one of the greatest places to be.

A Mama's Way

T*here is just* something *about a* mama's way of doing things.

You can ask a kid what he likes to eat and he can name the worst-sounding dish known to man. But as long as his mama cooks it, he'll eat it. Now, when he goes over to his friend's house, they could call that dish by the same name, make it with the same ingredients, and you can bet it won't taste as good. Because his friend's mama doesn't cook it like *his* mama does!

My mama would know that I hadn't cleaned up my room before she even looked. All she had to do was see the expression on my face. A mama can read volumes in just a single glance at her child's face.

I can be driving down the road, focusing straight ahead and listening to Shelby talk, and say to him,

"Shelby, get your fingers out of your mouth!" He'll look so surprised and say, "How'd you know I had my fingers in my mouth?"

"Oh, mamas just know these things." I like to keep him in suspense.

A mama knows, somehow, what you're doing even when she can't see you! That has puzzled more kids in this world than the wizardry of all the magicians put together! The strange thing is, I don't remember any special wave of a magic wand or some puff of smoke that suddenly turned me into one of those mamas. It just seemed to happen as soon as I got the job.

Of course, no matter how old a son or daughter gets to be, they turn into a five-year-old as soon as their mama walks through the door. I've been out on the road, feeling a little homesick, and as soon as I call home and Mama answers the phone, my homesickness multiplies tenfold. It's not really different from when I was in the ninth grade and I got the opportunity to participate in a basketball camp in Wahoo, Nebraska. I rode up with two basketball coaches and two other players all the way from Lindsay, Oklahoma. We drove all night long, and when we got there at dawn the next morning, the first thing I did was call Mama.

I was crying on my end of the line and she was doing her best not to cry on her end. But after talking to her, I knew I could do it. I could stay up at the basketball camp for three weeks. I just needed to talk to her. She encouraged me to stay, although she probably knew that if she had said the right words, I would have asked if I could get right back in the car and go home!

When you're the least bit sick, who do you want taking care of you? Mama!

When Narvel and I were in London on our first official European tour and had been gone for about ten days, I called home just as Shelby was getting ready for school. I said, "Hey, buddy! How are you doing this morning?"

He said in a small, pathetic whimper, "Mom, my stomach hurts."

"How come, Shelby?" I asked him.

"I don't know," Shelby said.

"Oh, honey, I wish I was there to rub it for you and make it okay," I said, trying to make it better over the phone.

"Me too," he said, still talking real sadlike.

Now, right beside me, Narvel heard what was going on and said, "It must be his new hairdo."

So I said, "You know what your daddy said?"

And, of course, once he heard his daddy mentioned, he was back to talking in his big-boy, normal voice and asked, "*What?*"

Daddies can know just the right thing to say too!

Although . . . you do always wind up seeing *a whole lot* of your mama in yourself. It seems like the older you get, the more you sound like her, answer the phone like her, give those disgusted looks like her, call for your kids playing outside like her, and, most of all, you find yourself raising your kids just like she raised you.

There's just nothing stronger or more lasting than a good mama's influence, that special sense of security when she's around that you can still pull close to you for comfort when she's physically far away. I hope Shelby always feels that same way when I'm with him. I know how hard it is to leave home. I also know how hard it is to move to another state and be that far away from Mama. And now, even though Shelby is (I hope) a long way from leaving home, I can appreciate how hard it was on my mama when I left.

Mama has always been a very strong woman. And I think the reason she understood better than anyone else why I had to move to Nashville was that she herself had wanted to go off to California when she was younger and pursue her music career. Unlike me, she didn't have anyone there encouraging her to go on with her dreams. No one to drive her to her dream destination. She treated me like she wished someone had treated her.

That was Mama's own golden rule, to do for us kids what she wished had been done for her. If Mama missed out on something in life, she tried her hardest to make sure that loss was not handed down to the next generation.

Like most of Mama's ways, I'm awfully glad she passed on that tradition to me, and even though he won't be a mama, I know it's my duty, my responsibility, and my pleasure to pass on the best of Mama's teachings to Shelby each and every day.

Set a Spell

While *it's true that I love* to have something to do at all times, there are those times when it does not take much convincing to get me to sit back and "set a spell." Just sitting around is too often an overlooked pleasure in our hectic world of today.

I love to rock in a rocking chair. Some of my most cherished, indescribably precious moments when Shelby was a baby came when I would sit and rock him for as long as I could. His two A.M. feedings were my favorite. Most mothers won't think that's weird at all. Narvel loved that I loved it so much so he could sleep through the night, but he had no idea what he was missing. I would sit and listen to the radio and rock Shelby while he drank his formula. When I tell him about my trying to take the bottle out of his mouth when he would fall asleep, which would make him quickly latch back on again, it makes Shelby giggle out loud.

I think I'll definitely be a rocker when I get older. And I will probably enjoy it so much that I will think that expression "you're off your rocker" will only apply to those people who are crazy enough not to be rocking along with me.

Porches, porch swings, and rocking chairs go together. We used to go down to a ranch in Post, Texas, where they put on a steer roping each year. Daddy's won it several times and Pake has also. On the ranch, of course, they had a beautiful old ranch house. The house was shaped in a square with a porch all the way around it. The banisters were painted white. I loved that old house, and I have loved porches ever since.

Grandma's house had a small front porch, and in the evenings when we were over there, we would sit on the porch swing and bench and help Grandma churn butter from the milk Grandpa had gotten from the cow that evening. We would sit and watch the sunset and holler toward the hills across the road and wait for the echo to return.

But for total abandoned kicking back, I do like a hammock. Right after Shelby was born, Narvel bought me a huge hammock with a wooden stand for it to hang on so it could be moved anywhere on our place. We love it and use it still.

Even in the most faraway places, I have sent my

spirits soaring simply by lying back in an unexpected hammock. I filmed a video for "And Still" in a small town four hours outside of Guatemala City. We stayed in a nice, clean cabin motel on the outskirts of a town overlooking a beautiful lake that sat between two dormant volcanoes. On the porch of my cabin was a hammock. What a treat it was to come back from a hard day of filming in such a remote place and be able to sink right down into the simple comfort of that hammock.

Rocker, porch swing, or hammock—you don't have to ask me twice!

Peanut Butter and Jelly

Yeah, but can you make a peanut butter and jelly sandwich? I often hear people say, "I wish I had your talent, I can't do anything like you can." You'd be amazed what you can learn from people who think they have no talent. Everyone has a talent. They might not think so, but they do. I believe God gave everybody a talent; you just have to look for it.

My housekeeper before Kimmie, Rose Carter, who took great care of us for five years, had many great talents. She was an immaculate housekeeper and she was learning to be a nutritionist. She kept me supplied with fresh-squeezed juice in the morning, carrot juice at noontime, barley, green and fresh vegetables. But the one thing that has saved me many times since Rose left was knowing how to make a great peanut butter and jelly sandwich. That's what Rose taught me. No matter how many songs you can sing, how many paintings you can paint, how many great marketing plans you can create, when your child looks up with those great big brown eyes, you'd better be able to make a great peanut butter and jelly sandwich!

So I'll share my secret with you. You *mix* the peanut butter and jelly (Shelby prefers grape jelly and creamy peanut butter) together before you put it on the bread! It makes it creamier! And it's better if the bread is not toasted. You think this is funny? Wait till your little one looks up at you and you'll be digging through this book, looking for my never-fail peanut butter and jelly sandwich recipe.

But no matter how insignificant you think your talent is, just know that out there in that big ol' world there are people who can't do what you can do. So use and share your talent to the best of your ability and be proud of it. Because God gave it to you.

Pulling Teeth

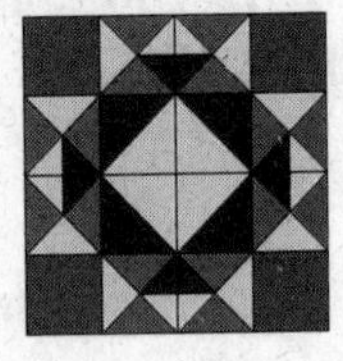

I*t's the tiniest little thing, but* don't we all make the biggest fuss over our kids' losing their first tooth. I think this might be one of the first times a child gets a sense that the big people have lost all sense of what it means to be little. Certainly, in our family, there's some evidence that the kids would do a whole lot better without our help and advice.

The other day Shelby brought home a book from school he had to read as a homework project. It was about a little monkey who had a loose tooth. His mother was trying to get him to be brave and let her pull it. He refused.

While Shelby was reading the story to me, I got so tickled that Shelby and Chelsea stopped and stared at me. I had to stop the reading and tell them the story about Trevor.

Trevor is my sister Alice's youngest son and is now in high school. When he was a little boy about five years old, he, like all five-year-olds, started losing his teeth. Now, Trevor is all boy and he loves his daddy! If his daddy suggested pulling his tooth a certain way, Trevor would more than likely try it. And that's exactly what happened!

Alice said they were in the living room, watching TV, when they heard a loud scream! Trevor had been in his room for quite a while and had gotten some string and tied it to his tooth and onto the doorknob. Then he reared back and slammed a door.

I had heard people talking about doing that all my life, but Trevor is the only person I know who willingly pulled his own tooth by slamming a door. Just following his daddy's suggestion. I never would have gotten up the nerve to *close* the door, much less *slam* it! I sure wish I could have taken a picture of his face. I really don't think he realized what was going to happen.

But on Shelby's first loose tooth, I was ready. Rose Carter, our housekeeper at the time, kept a close watch on Shelby's progress. Thank God I was home when Rose announced that it was time to pull the tooth. Shelby had moved it with his tongue, his finger, had eaten apples for days, and had done everything he could think of to get that tooth out. He had heard about the tooth fairy and was eager to see how much money he might get.

So I got the movie camera and still camera out and was ready for the grand production! Rose lay Shelby down on the kitchen floor and pulled out a long string of dental floss. She wrapped the dental floss around Shelby's tooth, and before Shelby realized what was going on, Rose pulled on the dental floss in opposite directions and out came the tooth!

Shelby was very proud of this accomplishment. He stood with his mouth open so I could take pictures.

But that was the last time anyone other than the oral hygienist got close to him with dental floss!

The latest "tooth puller" in our family is Chelsea! When we went on our Christmas vacation this past December, Chelsea had a loose front bottom tooth with one growing in behind it. We had all tried our best to get her to let us pull it, or help her pull it, but to no avail! So one night we were eating at our favorite Mexican restaurant, when she told her mother that she had to go to the bathroom.

We all sat around the table, waiting. Finally, Harley, her daddy, said, "Chas, would you go see what's happened to my girls?"

So Chassidy went to the rest room to check on Shawna and Chelsea. She came back shortly with a grin on her face and said, "They'll be right here."

Sure enough, here came Chelsea, also grinning from ear to ear, a paper towel stuck in her mouth. Of course we all wanted to know what happened.

Shawna said, "We got in the bathroom and Chelsea wanted to look at her loose tooth. So I picked her up and sat her on the vanity so she could see in the mirror. Then she wanted a wet paper towel, and when I gave her one, she put it over her tooth and pulled it out!"

I guess she just decided it was time to take matters into her own hands—and she did. We all applauded Chelsea, and you've never seen a more proud five-year-old in your life!

Several years ago Brandon came to live with us. He had to have his wisdom teeth pulled. Narvel took him to an oral surgeon and the doctor told them he was pulling the two bottom teeth, so Brandon would be put to sleep for a short time for the surgery. He also gave Narvel a prescription for pain medication, saying that once Brandon got home and the anesthesia wore off, he was to take the medication to control the pain.

The doctor said the best thing we could do when he got home was to keep ice on his jaw to keep the swelling down. Brandon was so out of it, he had no idea what we were doing to him. The way he felt, I don't think he would have cared.

His little sister, Chassidy, had had her wisdom teeth pulled several months earlier, and I had used the same home remedy on her. Rose Carter had let me in on a good way to keep ice on the jaw to prevent swelling. We took two sponges, about four by six inches, got them pretty wet, and put them in the freezer the day before the surgery. When we took them out of the freezer, we let them thaw just enough to conform to Brandon's jaw.

Now, the question is, how do you keep the sponges up against his jaw while he sleeps?

Panty hose!!

Yep! I tied a knot at the top of a clean pair of panty hose, put a sponge in each leg, resting right on the inside of the thigh part, put the crotch part under his chin, and then tied the legs in a knot on top of his head.

With Brandon out of it, we sat around him laughing and joking about taking pictures of him in his incapacitated condition. Of course we didn't, I don't think. Oh, well, that's what we told Brandon, anyway!

Let a Smile Be Your Umbrella . . . but Don't Forget Your Raincoat

Y*ou know that saying "Let a* smile be your umbrella"? Well, as seriously as we take our concerts, it always keeps us lively when we can put some fun into our regular routine. And, indeed, there was one time when I had one of my biggest laughs and, believe it or not, it involved the unexpected appearance of not an umbrella but a raincoat. But I'm getting ahead of my story.

Actually, I think there's a great country tradition of practical jokesters, tricksters, and goofy folks. On the ranch you always had to keep an eye out for somebody messin' with you just for fun.

It's said that anybody who's too busy to laugh is indeed too busy. Because they are such rascals, in addition to being such terrific performers, Brooks & Dunn are among the artists I have most enjoyed touring with. I absolutely love working with these two guys, and we've toured together for four years. But when you hang out with Ronnie and Kix—watch out! You just know they're going to get you. It's only a matter of when, and whether you'll be devious enough to get them back.

Kix and Ronnie are notorious for their practical jokes. One year when they were touring with Jo Dee Messina, she filled their bus completely with helium balloons! So Kix kidnapped Jo Dee one night, put her in a limousine, and drove her around the coliseum where they were performing, and knowing how fond she was of balloons, put her in the basket of a *hot air balloon*! Jo Dee is petrified of heights! She almost jumped out. Kix came out the loser in this battle. She almost whipped him!

Ronnie and Kix opened the show for me the first two years, in '92 and '93. Then they started headlining, and it wasn't until '97 that we got back together to share the stage. We all decided it would make sense and be a bigger and better show for the fans if we joined forces and toured together. Both of us being headliners, we decided to flip-flop closing the show each night. That meant on Friday night I would close the show and they would open. The next night I would open the show and they would close. It worked out really well.

Of course, everyone said it would never work, two headliners working together, but it did! Then, because of the song "If You See Him, If You See Her," we toured together again in 1998.

On our 1997 tour, after the last song of whoever was closing the show was over, that act would leave the stage and the lights would go out. If I had just finished, I would change clothes while Ronnie would go up onstage and start singing the Mickey Gilley song "You Don't Know Me." I would then come up on the elevator and join Ronnie on the second verse of the song. As soon as our song was over, we'd talk a little about how much we enjoyed singing with each other. Then I'd say how nervous I was about a certain third party not being where I could see him.

I had good reason to be more than a little uncomfortable about Kix's whereabouts! But sure enough, the fireworks would go off and he would appear at the end of the stage, performing "Cotton Fields." When he would get closer to Ronnie and me, we'd all be singing together, both bands would be playing together, and we'd have a great time! It was a great finale.

Well, one night during "Cotton Fields," Kix and I were singing the second verse face-to-face. Kix, of course not intentionally, sort of sprayed me with saliva while he was singing. When we got through and took our bows and got offstage, I hollered at Kix. "Would you stop spitting in my face?!"

Ronnie said, "Did he do that?"

I said, "Yeah!"

Of course Kix was apologizing over and over.

The next night, when I got to my dressing room, on my door hung a brand-new yellow raincoat with a hood and yellow rain pants to match. I thought that was hysterical! Sandi suggested that I make good use of it. So I did!

Sandi, my stylist, and I had it worked out that right before the second verse I'd walk around on the opposite side of the stage from Ronnie and Kix and Sandi would hand me the raincoat.

I slipped it on and walked up to Kix, face-to-face, to sing. You should have seen the look on his face! It was priceless!

They flew back to Nashville with me that night, and we laughed about the raincoat all the way home.

And I'm sure there were thirteen thousand people driving home that night after the concert wondering to themselves, Of all the costumes Reba could have worn . . . ?

Last fall in State College, Pennsylvania, we were doing our usual preconcert meet'n'greet, and Ronnie brought along one of those gag "fart" machines under his jacket. Every time someone handed him a picture to sign, he'd push the remote control and let 'er rip! Some acknowledged it, some didn't.

Sandi hadn't seen what was going on. She was busy getting people moved up in the line, taking cameras so Doug Nichols, Brooks & Dunn's media coordinator, could take their pictures. When she walked up to Ronnie holding a T-shirt for him to sign, he hit the remote.

At first it didn't register on her face that she had heard anything out of the ordinary. Then a surprised look on her face told us she knew exactly what she had heard. It certainly is a shock to realize that someone has passed gas in polite company. You don't know whether to ignore it or to acknowledge it.

Too late for Sandi! Kix and I were already rolling on the floor, laughing at her reaction.

Hey, I never said we were sophisticated in our choices of humor and practical jokes, but when you're far from home and working as hard as we do, it sure feels good to let loose with a good ol' gut-bustin' belly laugh whenever and however you can.

Just Listen

I*'ve never been accused of being* a quiet person. I was always the loudmouth of the bunch, the cutup, the one craving attention. Anytime I was quiet, I was either asleep or sick. But now there are many times when I value the importance of just concentrating or listening to somebody or something other than myself.

I can't express how important it is to be a good listener. I have to concentrate when I'm listening to demonstration tapes trying to find songs for my next CD. If I don't, I might miss a song I'd love to sing for the rest of my life! The ability to really focus and concentrate is not something I was born with. Mama always said I had the attention span of a two-year-old. So since that time, I've had to train myself.

I know I can't listen to songs when anything around me is distracting me. So my favorite time to listen is when I'm driving in my car, all by myself. When someone is in the car with me, I'm worrying if the volume is too loud, if they like it or not, or if they think I'm crazy for listening to that certain song so long. It's very important for me to focus on the music. It's my business, my livelihood, and I absolutely love it! I can listen to demo tapes for hours at a time. I'm always so curious when the next great song is going to come along.

Listening to someone when they speak to me is also very important. I know immediately when someone I'm talking to is either thinking about what he or she is going to say next when I'm through talking or truly listening to what I have to say. It's very rude not to listen to your speaker. It's also cheating yourself. You might learn something. If you're not listening, then you're missing out on an opportunity to find out what's going on.

Being a good listener sometimes means you're a better friend. When I have a problem I'm trying to deal with and I share it with someone I trust, I don't expect an answer. I don't expect the listener to fix anything. I just need an ear! So next time you are required to listen to music or to a friend, stop, think about it, and concentrate. Then do your best to lend an ear. You won't regret it!

Songs

When *I first got started in* Nashville, many singers, especially "girl singers," didn't have a say in what they were going to record. The record label executives and producers made those decisions. At the beginning I was very willing to go along with this because they knew a lot more than I did about procedures and how to select great songs to record. But after seven or eight years of watching and learning I won the right to select my own songs, so, like any freedom you fight for, this one is especially precious and important to me.

When I look for songs for a new album, I spend months listening to hundreds upon hundreds of demo tapes, rough recordings made by the songwriter and demo singers.

It's often that crucial first listening, when I am just like my fans, eagerly hoping to hear something that will capture my attention first, and then, if it's one of those rare, truly exceptional songs, will sweep away my emotions and my heart even in its rough form.

"Somebody Should Leave" is such a sad song. I'll never forget the first time I heard it. Harlan Howard is one of the most successful veteran songwriters in Nashville. I was honored to even have listening time with him. I sat in a leather wing chair and he played me some songs, and I was kind of curious why he was playing me songs that sounded so ordinary. I looked over at him and he was just looking off in the distance.

He stopped the tape and said, "What did you think?"

I said, "Harlan, I'm going to pass on that one." And he smiled and played another one and I said I was going to pass on that one too. And he grinned some more and said, "I think I got you one now."

What he was doing was playing those other songs to test me. If I had taken the first few songs, he never would have played me "Somebody Should Leave," which he wrote with Chick Raines. He wanted to know if I knew the difference between a good song and a mediocre song. It was a good lesson in sticking to your instincts no matter who's testing you!

When he played "Somebody Should Leave," tears came to my eyes and chills covered my body all over. And when he stopped the tape player, he grinned. I said, "Harlan, can I have that song?"

He said, "You got it!"

Back in 1993, I had listened one day to everything the folks at one of the publishing companies, Blue Water Music, had to offer. Then they said, "Now,

Reba, we have an unusual song and we're not even sure you'll want to listen to it all the way through, but it's cowritten by Sandy Knox and Steve Rosen and we know you like Sandy's writing."

So they played me "She Thinks His Name Was John," and the first time I heard it, I knew it was a song about AIDS and it didn't dawn on me that there had not been any songs out in country music dealing with AIDS. I didn't think about whether this was a hot, controversial topic. I just knew that it moved me as a great, well-written story song.

It was only after I brought it home to Narvel that I began to realize that this was a powerful song whose message very much needed to be talked about.

We recorded it for the *Read My Mind* album, and soon the radio program managers from around the country called up MCA and said their listeners who had listened to the album were demanding to hear the song played on the air. MCA urged us to release the song as a single.

I commend the listeners and the radio executives for standing up for a song like this and saying that this is a subject that we need to get out of the dark and something we need to talk to one another about.

That's why I respect fine songwriters like Sandy Knox. They can weave together a few seemingly simple thoughts with words everyone can relate to and get us to deal with sometimes painful subjects and emotions in our everyday life that might prove uncomfortable or even impossible to deal with in straight conversation.

I first came to know about Sandy Knox when I got a call from a good friend of ours, Leigh Reynolds. He had found a song that he wanted me to listen to. A good friend of his had written it; her name was Sandy Knox. It was called "He Wants to Get Married" and she wrote it with Anthony Little. The hook of the song was in the last line, so Leigh made sure I listened to the whole song and not just a verse and a chorus. I loved it so much that I immediately put the song on hold and later recorded it.

Sandy is a great writer. She writes unusual songs that have messages to them and really hit your heart when you listen to them. She brought me several more songs after that, like "Does He Love You" and "Why Haven't I Heard from You" that I recorded, but the one that has most affected me is "She Thinks His Name Was John," a song she wrote for her brother, Danny. Danny had cancer and during his illness needed a blood transfusion. From that he contracted AIDS. He fought, suffered, and spent as much time with his family as he could. Sandy and Danny were very close. So that would explain why it was so important for her to write a song for Danny. It was a tribute to him, his life, and what he had gone through.

It took her several years to hone in on the one line that would make the song work the way she wished, because Sandy didn't want the song to mention death or AIDS or to point a finger or preach to anyone. She wanted to make a statement, and a strong one she did. She felt that if the song made anyone think before having unprotected sex, then her mission had been successful.

That song made a huge impact on a lot of folks who came to my show and those who heard me sing it on TV.

I think it's very important for me to choose songs that get people to think. Songs hit home for folks when they can relate to the subject matter in the song.

Another song that I fell in love with is "The Greatest Man I Never Knew," by Richard Leigh and Layng Martine, Jr. I could really relate to this song. It's a song about a man who was not comfortable saying I love you to his children. My daddy never said I love you to any of us kids, just like the man in the song never expressed his feelings to his child. It's not that he didn't love us, he just didn't like saying it. Unfortunately, that was a common occurrence among men in my parents' generation. It made some men very uncomfortable. Emotions were left to the mothers to express. I've seen women, men, and their children sit there in my audience and cry during that song.

And then there is "Fancy." Sometimes after I sing "Fancy," I tell my audience, "Thank you for letting me sing my favorite song. I've loved it ever since Bobbie Gentry wrote and recorded it back in 1968." There is something about the raw drive of that character, about her hunger to triumph over the hard knocks her family has been through, that makes it the anthem of anybody, but especially any woman who feels mistreated. I know it gets my blood stirring no matter how many times I perform it!

But probably no song I have ever recorded has had an impact on women's lives like "Is There Life Out There," by Susan Longacre and Rick Giles. When I sing that song, women stand up all over the arena. It's their anthem! I'm singing that song for them! They are the women who after their children have left home go to college and get their degrees. They have another goal in life. They have raised their children, taken care of their home, and now it's their turn to do something for themselves.

I'm always looking for more songs that I can record for the next CD. I'm just like my fans. I can't wait to hear that next new song that will knock me out, that I'm passionate about, that I can't get out of my head, that I can't wait to sing!

Heroes

When *I was a kid, my* heroes were John Wayne and Joe Namath. I had their posters up in my bedroom and even in my college dorm room, along with one of Secretariat, the famous racehorse. It's funny how when you grow up, your ideas of heroes change. Now my heroes consist of people who may not be in the spotlight but are good, honest people with uplifting morals.

Outside of my family, two of my favorite people are President and Mrs. George Bush. We were scheduled to perform at the Houston Livestock Show and Rodeo in 1997, when we got an invitation to have lunch with them at their home there in Houston. Narvel and I were very nervous about going but wouldn't miss the opportunity. We later agreed that it was just like going over to an old friend's house.

I didn't have to keep reminding myself where I was or whose house I was in because the pictures of the things that the Bushes had gotten to do over the years were everywhere. It wasn't an elaborate house but very nice. It was very livable and comfortable. On the living room floor was a cross-stitched rug that Mrs. Bush had handmade during President Bush's campaign for president. It was beautiful.

While we were having drinks before lunch, Barbara asked if we'd like to see their new swimming pool. "Sure!" we said.

"Well, the only way you can see it is from our bathroom window," she said.

So as President Bush led us out of the living room up to their bedroom, Barbara said, "Could you make the bed while you're up there?" Of course it was already made. She was always cutting jokes like that and saying things that made you feel right at home.

In their bathroom we had to look out the window that was over the toilet to see their new swimming pool. It was one of those exercise pools where the jets blow on you so you can swim in place.

Lunch was wonderful, soup and salad. Nothing fancy but very filling. President Bush had to catch a plane for another engagement he had that evening. He might not be president anymore, but that doesn't mean he's not busy. He had just spoken in Denver the night before and wasn't able to come to our show that night because of having to leave Houston that afternoon.

He had attended the rodeo the year before and had come by my dressing room before my show just to say hi. That meant the world to me.

When Bush was president, Narvel, Shelby, and I were invited to the White House. Shelby wasn't even a year old, and it was the thrill of a lifetime for us. I'll never forget Shelby sitting on President Bush's lap, holding on to the president's thumb and slobbering all over it! President Bush just laughed and said, "Oh, that's okay, my grandkids do that all the time!"

When we left the Oval Office, we were walking down the hall, going back to meet our escort, when Barbara called out to us and asked if we'd like to see where they lived. She took us up to their apartment, to the Kennedy Bedroom and the Lincoln Bedroom. Shelby even got to pet Millie, who ran up the stairs instead of taking the elevator with us.

Also in 1997, we were the guests of Jerry Jones, owner of the Dallas Cowboys, at a Cowboys, football game. I sang the national anthem before the game and then went up to Jerry's suite. And guess who else was there? President Bush. I sat with him for a little while, watching the game and visiting. I looked over and he was eating fried chicken and having a glass of milk. How much more American can you get?!

Other heroes of mine are doctors, nurses, volunteer

workers, and firemen. But my biggest heroes of all are teachers. They hold our future leaders in their hands. They have the attention of those children a lot more than we parents do. So the responsibility of a teacher is tremendous! I applaud them! I respect them and I admire their courage. I think they are underpaid and underappreciated. My mother and grandmother were teachers and I have my degree in elementary education, though I have never taught since I completed my student teaching. I'd like to think I would have been a fine teacher just like Mama. I know I would be proud to be thought of as one, and, who knows, maybe someday I will get back to teaching. That threat should be incentive enough for all the students in the states of Oklahoma and Tennessee to keep buying my CDs so I'll be sure to stay in the music business!

So let's keep our heroes! Let's keep them up on a pedestal, where they belong! Let's keep encouraging them so they continue to do their great work. We need them. They're also great role models for our children, who need genuine heroes to look up to, to respect, and to admire, just like I did when I was a kid.

Real Courage

People ask me, *"How do you* have the courage to get up onstage and sing in front of all those people?"

That's definitely not my idea of courage. But, of course, I'm used to it by now and it's been a long time since my knees have knocked together before a show. Doing what I do onstage is a matter of overcoming fear and insecurity and learning to trust the confidence in my God-given ability to perform and trust in my performing team to back me up.

Real courage to me is when a parent is looking her child in the eye, knowing that her child is dying of cancer yet able to reassure that child in his final days that everything is okay, and then has to struggle to keep the rest of the family together.

Courage to me is a doctor or nurse walking into

the hospital day in and day out, taking care of sick and injured people.

Courage to me is a teacher getting up out of bed every weekday morning knowing that what he or she does and says that day to the students could make a difference and change a child's life forever.

Courage to me is the policeman laying his life on the line every time he walks on duty.

Courage to me is a man and a woman making the decision to have a child. That's taking responsibility with a capital R that no one can even fathom until that child is born.

At our shows we do a backstage program that invites people to come and meet me. We call it a meet'n'greet. We always honor a request from the Make-A-Wish Foundation for someone on their list to come backstage. Sadly, it's usually their last wish.

One night we were just about finished with the backstage visits. I was about to go onstage for my performance, when in walked the cutest little blue-eyed, blond-haired girl I'd ever seen. I talked to her, signed a picture for her, and visited longer with her than with anyone else all night. She was so personable and talked up a storm. I didn't know until her parents walked up that she was from the Make-A-Wish Foundation. That's when they told me she had four months to live. I reached down, hugged her, and they all walked out the door and out of my life.

For the next four months those parents would have to demonstrate the largest amount of courage they could muster.

That's real courage.

For the past few years I've enjoyed hosting the Reba McEntire Pro Celebrity Rodeo: A Tribute to Ben Johnson, in Oklahoma City. A wonderful actor and horseman, the late Ben Johnson originally got me involved in this rodeo, which benefits the Children's Medical Research Hospital in Oklahoma City. We go to the hospital and visit the kids during the day. Then that night there is a wonderful dinner and auction at the Cowboy Hall of Fame to raise money for the hospital. The next morning the children come out to the Lazy E Arena in Guthrie, Oklahoma. They ride the stagecoach and a horse-drawn wagon around the arena, and all the celebrities, cowboys, and cowgirls sign autographs and take pictures with the kids. Then that night we put on a rodeo. It's all for fun and all to raise money for the kids.

When we visit the hospital, it hurts so much to walk from bed to bed, where the children lie with tubes coming out of their noses, arms, and mouths, their heads partially or completely shaved. It's hard to walk in and act like everything is as normal as can be. But, boy, is it worth it! To see the smiles on those beautiful little faces. It's priceless!

But we're at that hospital only one day of the year.

To me, the most courageous people in the world are the ones who go to the hospital every day to take care of those kids, knowing that some will never leave the hospital. I highly respect the doctors and nurses, and also the volunteers and folks who make it a point to go visit patients each week.

It also seems that along with courage goes a lot of love. Unconditional love. Love that feels great being given and not expecting any in return.

I've seen the parents of the children too. A daddy sitting at his little girl's bedside, stroking her arm while she sleeps. How do they do it?

There was a sign on Roy Acuff's dressing room door at the Grand Ole Opry that said:

Lord, grant me the serenity
To accept the things I cannot change,
Change the things I can, and
The wisdom to know the difference.

Thank God, He answers those prayers and gives courage to those who need it.

Getting There

T*he night I won the Country* Music Association Entertainer of the Year Award I was sitting in the limousine with Daddy afterward and I asked him what he liked most about winning the World Championship in Steer Roping. He said, "Getting there." I completely understood what he meant.

I certainly enjoy the professional position I am in today. I love getting to travel in first-class fashion. But I also look back with fond memories on all the baby steps that it took for me to get here. For instance, I thoroughly enjoyed being the only girl on the bus with my band members and driver, mainly because I was the boss! Ha!

I loved getting to open the show for Red Steagall and travel with him and the Coleman County Cowboys. Hearing the great road stories they'd tell was priceless! They watched over me like I was their little sister! I even look back with fondness on the times the bus would break down and all of us as a unit would have to figure out what to do.

See, it wasn't only the great, glamorous, star-studded times that I can write about being fun. I totally enjoyed the "getting there"! That means all the interesting things in between the "getting discovered" to "walking up the steps and accepting your first award."

I enjoyed the trips to Los Angeles and my first time in a limousine and my first time on Johnny Carson's *Tonight Show*. Even the bad hotel rooms were something to laugh about days later. It was mainly the camaraderie with my friends, sharing all the experiences that we went through, good or bad.

I also enjoyed getting to share all my newfound adventures with my family. It was a blast having Mama and Alice with me on one of my tours through Canada. Getting to see Banff in the Rocky Mountains is nothing to behold by yourself. It's a lot better when more oohs and aahs are heard than just your own!

I reflect back about awards I have won and about career milestones I have achieved. I realize it was usually the chase, the competition, the "getting there" that I thrived on, what I lived for. Each goal that was met only left me eager to set off on the journey to the next hurdle.

Now that I'm past forty and have had a music

career for nearly a quarter century, I find that some things have changed about my drive. I'm still what most people would consider driven and I still set my goals and standards as high as I can, but my drive has changed direction some because I've learned how to enjoy the journey a little more.

It's nice to be at a point in life where I don't feel quite as intense an urgency to constantly prove myself. I guess you could call it a sense of relaxation.

It's also a case of being more secure. Like I've always said, everyone wants to be loved and accepted, and security is born from that. I no longer seek to be accepted by everybody—a vital part of growing up is realizing that you can't please everyone. I have a great family, wonderful friends, songs to sing, and the ability to take my music and share it with anyone who wants to hear it.

It's new challenges of making videos and films, touring outside North America for the first time, competing with the wide array of fantastic young singers who keep coming into the business, that keeps my creative and competitive juices flowing. I now have the luxury of enough confidence in myself to apply some experience and perspective to my career decisions.

I am so fortunate to have friends from several generations of country music, from our living legends like Loretta Lynn and Dolly Parton, who taught me so much, to our spectacularly talented new stars like Trisha Yearwood and Martina McBride.

I am proud that maybe I have been able to contribute something to this business, and to the younger people just entering it. If something I went through makes it just a little easier on the next person, that's great. Isn't that what life is supposed to be about, making the path a little gentler for those traveling behind you? That's what Mama would say.

With a careful mixture of gratitude, experience, wisdom, and maturity, with youthful exuberance and the curiosity of a two-year-old, I feel certain that as I begin the rest of my journey, the most interesting and rewarding twists and turns lie ahead. I can't wait.

Getcha One Lick

I*'m very competitive! I like to* win! I've been that way since childhood. I came by it honestly; I'm a third-generation rodeo brat. My grandpap was the 1934 World Champion Steer Roper and my father won the Steer Roping championship in 1957, 1958, and 1961. Pake, my sisters, and I were raised around ambition and determination, which is the polite way of saying we're competitive and stubborn.

But wanting to be the best at everything was an unreachable, far-fetched dream for me.

Grandpap's words of wisdom directed to us kids were "Getcha one lick, master it, and go getcha another one!" At the time, he was referring to picking one event in rodeo, sticking with it long enough to master that event, and then picking another one to work on.

Eventually, I would come to appreciate that Grandpap was talking about life. But growing up, because I wanted to be everything from the world champion barrel racer, to the Country Music Association Entertainer of the Year, to a women's basketball star, those words of wisdom have been a long, hard lesson for me to learn. They have also focused me to have some good, honest chats with myself about accepting my limitations. But that took a while.

When I was a teenager, I was playing basketball, driving the hay-hauling trucks, and singing. Daddy walked by me one afternoon, stopping long enough for me to realize I had interrupted his routine. He said, "Reba, why do you always want to do something you can't do?" Of my confused and puzzled look, he said, "Why don't you just practice your singing?" I wanted to ask, How do you do that? but I knew better.

Singing, performing, and entertaining are my God-given talents that I can comfortably say I'm good at. And I've learned that all the other things I tried to do along the way, such as my own publicity, my own travel arrangements, scheduling, bookkeeping, wardrobe, management, hairstyling, housekeeping, needed to be handed over to capable people who are the best at what they do! Instead of attacking life's challenges head-on, I've had to force myself to surround myself with talented people who are good at the things I struggle with. So I've learned to delegate responsibilities to new people and trust their talent and wisdom. I've also had to learn to stay out of their territories the same way I needed them to stay out of mine.

Being a leader in business and an organization, I've learned that two of the most important things are to set examples for your fellow workers and to make sure that each individual is focused on his or her tasks, not somebody else's. If you give them a responsibility, talk about how you want the job done and then let them either do it your way, incorporate their way with yours, or find a better way of doing it. In the end you have to approve the method and then let them prove they can handle the job. Then securities on both sides will grow.

It's all worked out really well. I've realized there's nothing shameful about sticking to what I can do. I like a good challenge, but I won't be the best at everything I try. And that's okay with me, even as competitive as I am.

The truth is, there's a lot of things I'm not the best at. I can cook a few dishes, but I'm not a good cook. I'm not a great housekeeper either. I'm not real orderly when it comes to organizing, I'm more of a pack rat! I love sports, but I'm not a great athlete. I've always wanted to paint or draw, but I'm not a great artist. I love having a great show to perform, but I'm the doer, not the thinker-upper!

I like trying new things, but I realize I don't have to be good at everything I try. It's okay just to have fun. I've also learned that it's better to let a new subject or activity go if it's becoming too stressful, dangerous, or a problem.

I think Grandpap would be pleased that I've worked out a few licks for myself: singing, performing, being a mother and a respectful partner in marriage and business. These, along with endeavoring to communicate effectively with other people and trying to learn and grow in all the new facets of my life, are the things I feel I'm good at. I'm proud of myself for sticking with the things I can do and continuing to do them better. And being content to do the other things for a challenge but mostly for fun.

Be a Performer

S*o many times I'm asked by* young people, "How do you get into the music business?" or "What do I do to become a professional singer?" I always start by saying, "Get the best education you possibly can. Finish school, go to college. Then you'll be ready and more prepared for the education that the world has to offer you." The business world will still be there for you when you complete your academic education.

I knew a young man once who wouldn't go and apply for a construction job on a highway just three miles away from his home. He said he didn't want to work anywhere for minimum wage. He didn't have a job, but he didn't want to start at the bottom. That's what he thought minimum wage was—the bottom.

I know a lot of people look at what I do today and say, "I want to do what Reba does." It looks easy, glamorous, fun, exciting, adventuresome, and it always looks as if it came fast. *Never!!!!* Ask Terri Clark, Brooks & Dunn, Shania Twain, Barbara Mandrell, Dolly Parton, Alabama, Vince Gill, Neal McCoy, Red Steagall, or anyone else in the business. There are two things that never happen—things never come fast or easy.

All of us had to start at the beginning. That's a lot nicer way of saying at the *bottom.* There's nothing to be ashamed of by doing this. You have to start learning somewhere, might as well be at the beginning. And the more you learn, the more you grow. You'll start by doing the job the way others before you have done it. But then it is your responsibility to find a new and better way of doing your job. Be a pioneer like the ones before you. A saying in the movie and entertainment business goes "We started in the mailroom together." That was a beginning, learning the ropes, learning the business, watching, soaking up information, and seeing how things tick.

Young aspiring singers sitting in the audience see only the bright lights, the huge audience, the fancy costumes, and the fine-tuned choreography. I often wonder if they look beyond the performers onstage to consider the many other roles being played out backstage and behind the scenes by people who are just as passionate and rewarded by their work as I am by mine. The positions that need to be filled before a show can ever be presented to the audience are numerous. There are the writers who sit and write song after song, hoping each one will be the next monster hit. Then you have the publishers who represent the writers and who own the songs that the writers write. Their job is to get the songs to the artists so the artists will record them and, hopefully, they will be the songs that are performed on the radio and during a show. Then you have the producers who sometimes pick the songs for the artist to record, and often go into the studios and orchestrate the songs. All the people in that process are vitally important! The musicians, the engineers, the second engineers, the background singers, and the list goes on and on.

There are promotion people at the record labels, and their job is to go to local radio stations and convince program directors to play a particular song. Then the deejays at the radio stations play the music. There are retail people at the record company who distribute the cassettes and CDs to the stores so people can buy them. They are also responsible for negotiating with the store manager for the placement of the records and posters in the stores. There are people who manage the artist and coordinate everything mentioned above. There are the tour managers who are responsible for getting the artist, band, and crew from point A to point B. They also make sure the artist gets to the interviews and TV shows on time. There are people responsible for making the videos that you watch on television. There are the program directors at the video channels who determine which videos get played and how often.

At the show you have the riggers, the promoters, the production and stage managers, the carpenters, sound technicians, lighting technicians, accountants, bus and truck drivers, caterers, stylists, art directors, guitar technicians, keyboard techs, drum techs, and so on. The promoter calls to see if an arena is available. Once the arena is available, he negotiates the rent and other financial details that are involved in engaging the building for that day. Then the production manager contacts the steward, who is in charge of all the local stagehands, and discusses the amount of local labor that will be needed to put the show up. He decides what rate will be charged for the laborers. He contacts the caterer and determines what foods will be served throughout the day and at what times and negotiates the price.

You'll never see many of the people who are heavily involved in making an artist successful. You'll enjoy and reap the benefits of all their hard work, but you'll probably never meet them. But thank God they are there! Because without them I wouldn't be doing what I love so much to do at the level I get to do it! While my band and I are in the spotlight smiling and performing and receiving the applause, these people are in offices, backstage, and around the world, making sure their part of the teamwork is running smoothly.

Now, I want to add to this, that some of these behind-the-scenes folks can make as much or more money than the people you see onstage. These are very important positions and have a tremendous amount of responsibility. The financial reward is large if they are very good at their job. Most of the people in these positions first thought their career would be onstage, but after being in the business for a while, they found another avenue, like the ones I mentioned above, more interesting and fulfilling.

And it is a wonderful business! I've enjoyed it tremendously! The greatest thing about my job is that I love what I get to do day in and day out! To be truly successful, you have to be passionate about your career. That means you're not only great at your job but you love every minute of it and that makes you happy!

So go ahead and get your education and be ready for the wonderful opportunities the world has to offer. Find a job you love and you'll never have to "work" a day in your life!

Hard Work

I*f I didn't know any better,* I would say it was fated for the McEntires to settle in Oklahoma all those years ago because the state motto is "Work conquers all things."

Because back in Chockie, hard work was like a member of our family—it was always around. That's how Mama and Daddy raised us because that was how they were raised and their mama and daddy were raised before them! There weren't many other options. It was real simple: If you worked hard, you got to eat. And if you worked real hard, you slept real well at night. I don't think I appreciated all that great training back then, but it has prepared me for the things I have encountered in my life.

My great fellow Oklahoman Will Rogers had a memorable take on the subject: "What the country needs is dirtier fingernails and cleaner minds." It's sad to see so many people today thinking that the world owes them something, and their mouths are full of "gimmes."

You definitely like the apples more if you have to shake the tree, but I figure there must be so many great sayings about working because so many people try to slide by without doing their fair share, like "He's kind of like a blister—he don't show up until the work's all done."

Or, worse, sitting back and criticizing people who are doing the hard and dirty work. I especially like "Most knocking is done by people who don't know how to ring the bell."

When it comes to my music, I learned early on from Conway Twitty, Mel Tillis, and Marshall Grant, who manages The Statler Brothers, Red Steagall, and Mama and Daddy to treat all aspects of it like a business. If you treat your music like a business, it will take care of you forever. If you treat it like a party, the party dies out. The lights do come on and everybody has to go home.

Early on I set myself the goal of finding ways to be different, to stand out, and then to work my butt off to put it across to the public. I always had my eye on going the distance, building a career, earning the respect and loyalty of fans. That's why it turned out to be so appropriate that my very first single in 1976 was entitled "I Don't Want to Be a One-Night Stand."

There were lots of frustrations and setbacks along the way. Once, after a show where everything seemed to be messed up, I stormed back to my van and scowled, "Oh, that just makes me so mad, I can't hardly stand it."

My cousin Paula was sitting there and said, "Why don't you quit?"

I snapped, "Well, that's the stupidest thing I ever heard in my life. I'll never quit." Right there it dawned on me. "Reba," I said to myself, "quit your gripin' and quit bitchin' and go do something about it. You know you want to and you know you can."

I think "Thou shalt not whine" should be the eleventh commandment.

I can't resist two more of those great old sayings: "Failure is the path of least persistence" and "The dictionary is the only place where success comes before work."

Then there's my one essential rule for survival: **Work hard. When you're done, continue to work hard. When you're done with that, keep working hard!**

Going with Your Gut

T*he best decisions that I ever* made in my life happened when I went with my gut feelings. I can always feel what is right for me better than others can. If I go by my heart or my gut, I usually don't go wrong.

And not every decision is easy to make. But I think that somewhere deep inside, every one of us knows the right thing to do. That's certainly been true for me when I'm at a crossroads. Maybe it's intuition, or maybe it's God's way for a little voice within me to call out and show me the way. Whatever it is, if I trust it, I make the right choice.

I think the hardest decision I ever made was to leave my first husband, Charlie Battles. I heard the voice and had the gut feeling, but it took a while for me to make that move. As soon as I did, I knew it was right.

My marriage was in trouble, and I wasn't happy, and for a long while I didn't know what to do to feel better. I never bellyached about my problems, so my family didn't really know how unhappy I felt. I kept all the pain inside and pretended.

So instead of dealing with my troubled marriage, I'd avoid it. I'd stay out on the road longer than I had to just because I didn't want to come home. I knew that what I was doing was wrong, and that little voice inside me wasn't talking loud enough for me to stop and listen. Or maybe it was and I just wasn't listening!

Then, in 1987, Daddy was in the hospital—he was going to have triple bypass heart surgery. My inner feeling hit me hard enough for me to finally pay attention. I heard that little voice inside, and it said, "Go forward! Go on and don't look back!"

I had been reading my little white Bible in Daddy's hospital room and I looked up and asked Mama if she would please go downtown with me to talk to a lawyer. I filed for divorce the very next day.

My family stood by me throughout the ordeal of that divorce. They never wavered. My life improved instantly and has kept on growing and getting filled with good things. I followed my gut instinct. I did what my heart knew was best for me, and my heart was right.

Now, that's not to say it was easy or painless. Sometimes the best things for us are the hardest things for us to do. Just because it's hard doesn't mean it's wrong. I learned that too.

How can you have confidence in your decisions? I think if you're true to yourself and do what you believe is right, you'll have all the inner confidence you'll need to get through anything.

Living Life with a Passion

I *always try my best to have* compassion for others and passion for what I do. When something really matters to me, I try to show it. But sometimes, because of getting caught up in a hectic work schedule or the grind of everyday life, the most difficult thing is to keep passion alive in everything I do. That's hard and I have to continue to remind myself of that! The thing I notice about great entertainers, actors, mothers, and wives is they are extremely passionate in what they're doing. That seems to be a common denominator for successful people. *Passion!!!!*

Sharing or relaying the passion, passing it on, is also very important. If I'm loving a song when I'm singing it, the person listening to that song will feel that same passion. And if they tell someone about their experience, it's passed on again.

But it extends to other things as well.

Last year Narvel and I attended our son Shelby's blue and gold Cub Scout banquet. The boys were so handsome in their uniforms and very proud of the patches and pins they were receiving. Our speaker for the evening, was a Vietnam veteran who spoke of loyalty, pride, and the importance of believing in our country. He spoke of his fellow countrymen giving their lives for our freedom. When he pointed to our American flag, he choked up and became very emotional. I was very moved by his talk, as was every parent and teacher in the small gymnasium, all because this man was so genuinely passionate about his love for his country. He cared so deeply, I could feel it.

For me, it was an experience, an emotion, and a lesson. In my everyday life, I need to passionately show how much I care about what I do. Whether I'm performing, getting Shelby ready for school, or listening to my husband's description of his day at work, that passion has to show. It needs to show to the extent that the person on the other side feels it too.

It all boils down to getting as much out of life as I possibly can with all the passion that goes with it. Then giving it back with the love and respect it deserves.

Giving Back

G*iving is the most fun and* rewarding thing in life. It's fun to watch the faces of the people receiving, to see their reaction, to hear them speak after a surprise. Usually there are tears, sometimes joy and lots of laughter, and even a hug or two happens.

It doesn't matter where you live or who you think you are, if you are not giving some of your time to serve your community, then I think you will have a terrible loneliness and isolation in your life no matter how financially successful you might be.

That's right, I said your time, not your money. Don't get me wrong, donating as much money as possible to worthy causes is something all of us need to do as generously and as often as we can. But time is the most precious treasure we have, and no matter how wealthy you might be, you can't buy a twenty-fifth hour to a day, and no matter how poor you might be, you can donate yourself and your time to help someone even less fortunate.

My family's ranch background, of course, was always filled with the old western tradition of neighbor helping neighbor, and rodeo performers, most of whom would be struggling to scrape together the gas money to get to the next rodeo, have always been notoriously generous when it comes to helping a contender who was busted up or flat-out busted. The thought that you could be competing against him for the prize money later on never entered the picture.

But it's the country music family that I'm proud to say has the most wonderful traditions of helping out their community. There is a virtually endless list of performers who are constantly giving their precious time on and off the road to host or participate in fund-raising events, to visit hospitals, to use their celebrity to call attention to good causes.

As our Starstruck organization has grown, both Narvel and I have considered it vitally important to encourage all of our employees to take time to give back to the community, and we have a number of individual and corporate projects going on at any given time. I have personally gotten so much from working with the volunteers on some of our favorite projects, which have included Habitat for Humanity, Feed the

Children, the Texoma Medical Center, Reba's Ranch House, the Reba McEntire Center for Rehabilitation, and the Children's Medical Research Hospital in Oklahoma City.

I was so honored when the Salvation Army asked me to kick off their 1997 holiday kettle drive by singing at half-time of the Dallas Cowboys Thanksgiving game. I debuted the wonderful Diane Warren song "What If," which includes the wish that I so believe that "if everybody reached out with one hand," we could make so many things better together. I continued to be so moved by this song and this project that I made it the closing number of my 1998 concert tour, and in every city we could we contacted a local choir to join me onstage to sing it. Night after night it proved to be among the most thrilling and moving songs I've ever performed, and certainly one of the most important messages I've ever delivered.

In 1998 I was deeply honored—and shocked—to be sitting in the audience of the Nashville Network Music City News Country Awards, when I heard my name announced as the winner of the Minnie Pearl Award. This award is named after its first recipient, my beloved friend and one of the finest, funniest ladies to ever grace a stage, Miss Minnie Pearl, and it is presented annually for outstanding humanitarian and community contributions.

As I said between tears during my acceptance speech, that award meant the world to me, because I loved Minnie so very, very much and she was such an inspiration to me in so many ways. That award is about sharing and about giving back, and it is those two activities that heal hearts and make us better people. For the more we love and the more we give, the richer we are.

The *Family* Christmas Tree

I *love Christmas. It brings back great* memories to me at different times. I have the memory of singing my first solo behind a microphone at the Christmas program at my school in Kiowa, Oklahoma, when I was in the first grade. I can instantly conjure up the smells of Christmas dinner and I can also remember the words of some of my favorite Christmas songs even in the middle of summer! And I know the story of Jesus's birth by heart.

But there are some things that are better left alone. Because I have lately found out that people have funny ways and different opinions of how to decorate their Christmas trees. Some folks keep traditions and rituals how the tree should be properly decorated. That can cause problems.

Now, when I was a kid, there wasn't any set way

to decorate our tree. We just had fun doing it! All of us would pile in the pickup with Mama and Daddy and head to Rob Davis's place right past Grandpap's house. At Rob's there was the biggest thicket of cedar trees we had ever seen. Daddy taught us that you don't go for one of the trees that are in a bunch of other trees, you look for one standing out by itself. If it's by itself, that means the sun has been able to shine on the tree from all sides and the branches have grown out fully and evenly. So all of us kids would scatter and try to be the first to find the family Christmas tree. Once it was selected, Daddy would chop it down with the chopping ax, we'd load it in the back of the pickup truck, and away we'd go, back home. Mama had been collecting ornaments for years. Nothing ever matched, but we didn't mind. But she did have to buy new icicles every year.

A good friend of ours, Donna Wilson, was a senior at Kiowa High School. She came home with us quite often after school just to be with the family. She and Mama were great friends and all of us kids loved her too. So it would start out with Donna and Alice overseeing the decorating with all of the rest of us pitching in when we could. We'd decorate the tree and everyone would stand back and ooh and aah about how great it looked. Of course, us kids were wondering how many gifts would be underneath the tree for us later on!

The next day Mama would take all the decorations off the tree and let Susie and me redecorate it all by ourselves. We were real serious at first and loved our mission! But after a while we got bored with the project and started throwing the icicles on by the handfuls! They got quite messed up! Then after Susie and I would run off and play, Alice and Donna would come back and redo the tree for the third time! It wasn't the fanciest or the prettiest, but it was the busiest tree in Oklahoma at Christmastime!

When Narvel and I got married, our methods of decorating were totally different!

Narvel was raised in a very strict Pentecostal home. At that time the belief was that a Christmas tree in the home meant that you were worshiping an object instead of focusing on God. One of his childhood memories was driving by the town's doctor's house, which happened to be the biggest house in town with a huge bay window in the front. The doctor always had a gorgeous flocked tree with all the matching trimmings. Narvel thought it was the most beautiful thing he'd ever seen. His dream was to someday have a tree like the doctor's. So when Narvel and I started the project of getting our first Christmas tree together, I was in for quite a surprise!

First of all, we went downtown and *bought* our tree! Second, Narvel asked if they could *flock* it! I had no idea what that was! That's when they take a green tree and spray a white solution on the tree that makes it look like the tree has snow on it. Then, when we got it to the house, there was the tedious procedure of wrapping the lights carefully around each branch, making sure the cord was not seen starting at the top and going to the bottom so the plug was exactly at the wall socket. Now, when we did it in Oklahoma, we pretty much laid the light strings on the branches and occasionally attached the lights to the limb. They stayed where they landed!

Narvel and I then started cutting beautiful ribbons, tying each one, and making them into pretty bows. Each bow was evenly distributed on different branches all over the tree. Another new thing to me. Then came the ornaments. Narvel never used the kind of icicles Susie and I used. He got the long icicle ornaments instead.

It turned out beautifully! It was the most beautiful tree I had ever seen! No, it wasn't like any tree I had when I was a kid, but it wasn't like Narvel's childhood tree either. It was *our* tree. That's when I realized that each person has a very specific memory or dream of Christmas from childhood and likes to re-create or create that special time. But at the same time it's great to make new memories for the future together!

Soon after that we started ending our tour in the middle of December. That meant we were gone from home from Thanksgiving until Christmas. So we started hiring a very talented, patient lady to decorate the tree for us. Coming home to a beautifully decorated home was like walking into Disneyland at Christmastime. It was great! For those of you thinking Shelby gets left out of the Christmas decorating, I'll let you in on this little story. A couple of weeks before Christmas, when Shelby was three years old, he went to Oklahoma to spend a week with my family while we were touring. When we got Shelby back with us, Mama had put some pictures in his suitcase for us to see. One set of pictures was of Shelby decorating Mama and Daddy's Christmas tree. Mama had put some red ornaments around the top of the tree and had given Shelby the rest of them to put wherever he wanted. In a radius of about two feet, there must have been fifteen ornaments! That's as high as he could reach and as far as he wanted to move! It was so cute!

This past Christmas Narvel and I took all of our kids to Colorado. While we were sitting in the living room we got to admiring the Christmas tree and started talking about different Christmas tree experiences. It was funny because everyone had a funny story about putting up their tree. But Brandon and Melissa, who is Brandon's fiancée, had the funniest story. Melissa started telling it, but just like his father, Brandon had to take over the storytelling!

He told us that he and Melissa had been looking forward to Christmas, and they couldn't wait until Thanksgiving was over so they could go get their Christmas tree. They didn't want a store-bought tree, so they decided to go up to the three hundred acres that we own and select their own tree. It's a very dense and rough piece of land that requires a tractor to get into it. They also wanted it to be a very romantic and memorable day. So Brandon hooked the truck up to the flatbed trailer, drove the tractor up onto the trailer, and chained it all down securely. Brandon's nerves were wearing a little thin, but he remembered that this would become a day they would never forget. So he talked himself back into a good mood and off they drove to the three hundred acres. When they got there, Brandon had the task of loosening the chains, unloading the tractor, and climbing up into the cab of the tractor. Once again it was a grueling, time-consuming task, but he knew it was worth it. Melissa asked where she was going to sit. Brandon motioned to the wheel cover and said, "You can sit right here." Melissa sat down and after a second or two said, "Oh, that hurts! I don't like sitting here!" So Brandon got her over on his lap, which was more comfortable for Melissa, but it was getting very difficult for Brandon to see where he was going. Finally they got over to the thicket of cedar trees and climbed down out of the cab of the tractor. Brandon said, "Okay, let's go over there to the . . ." "Over there? I've got my good clothes on! I don't want to walk out into the brush!" Melissa said.

Brandon, looking a little surprised, said, "Did you think the perfect tree was going to be right here on the side of the road?" So finally Melissa gave in and hiked over to where Brandon thought the best tree was. She found just the one she wanted. Just as Brandon was cutting into it, he heard her say, "Oh! Wait a minute! This one over here is a lot prettier!" So over Brandon went to the other tree, and just as he was raising the chain saw to start the procedure, Melissa said, "You know, all of these trees look awfully brown! I don't see any tree that's nice and green." The trees were brown because of the drought we'd had the last part of the summer. She was right, they weren't very green. So, in not quite as good a mood as before, they drove the tractor back to the truck and trailer. Brandon got everything loaded and chained back down, and they headed back to the barn, where Brandon unloaded and replaced all the equipment.

Reluctantly, they went to Wal-Mart to *buy* a

Christmas tree. As they were looking at the trees, Melissa found a Christmas village she wanted desperately. So they got the tree and the village and home they went. Melissa wanted to assemble the village first, but Brandon wanted to put the tree up. Brandon won this one. Melissa had her way of putting the lights on the tree, Brandon had his way (his father's way, if the truth was known). Melissa won this one. So while Melissa was putting the lights on the tree, Brandon sat fuming while watching TV but watching Melissa string the lights out of the corner of his eye. The day wasn't turning out at all like either one of them had wished it would! When Melissa got through with the lights, she started trimming the tree with some trimmers. Brandon saw one branch that needed trimming really badly, but Melissa kept overlooking it. Brandon couldn't stand it any longer. He hopped up off his chair, went over and grabbed the trimmers from Melissa, and cut the branch that was driving him crazy. When he did, he cut right through a strand of the Christmas tree lights!

To say the least, it was not the kind of memorable day they were wishing for, but it was a Christmas they will never forget!

Jesus Loves Me

Oh! How I love Jesus
Oh! How I love Jesus
Oh! How I love Jesus
Because He first loved me.

T*here was a very small* one-room church in Chockie, Oklahoma, where I grew up. It was just over the railroad track and highway from our house. We seldom had anyone to play the piano for us while we sang our songs, so Mrs. McGee would hum a starting tone and we'd all sing the hymn in that key.

I can't say I overly enjoyed going to church in Chockie, but I did enjoy getting up in front of the small congregation, usually around twenty to thirty people, and singing with the members of the church. Once in a while Grandma and Grandpa, Mama's parents, would get up and sing a solo together. My favorite song was "Oh! How I Love Jesus." But my favorite place to sing it was not in the little Chockie church. My favorite place was sitting on the pond dam with Grandma while we were waiting for the fish to bite. That's also where she would tell us the stories from the Bible.

I've thought a lot about my time sitting on that pond dam. I had everything—peace, comfort, security, and family. But nothing made me feel more secure and loved than when I was wrapped in the arms of Jesus. It's happened several times in my life. It's so loving, so warm, and so comforting. It doesn't last long, I guess, because He has so many that need that special hug. But it's unforgettable!

In January of 1999, after two weeks of vacationing with the family, we took off for our first official tour of Europe. Our last show in the States had been December 13, so I was a little rusty on all the lyrics and changes of the show. Narvel and I had also worked on my talks in between each song so I could tell the story of my life and my music to my new audience in Europe.

Our opening night was in Glasgow, Scotland. I had been cramming, almost like a college exam, trying to remember all the words and everything in correct order. I sat in the bathroom there in the Glasgow Music Hall all by myself, talking to God, asking

Him, one more time, for His help. He gives me confidence. I love talking to Him. I don't need to be in a church, I don't need to be around others to watch me worship. I need the privacy so I can give my undivided attention to my Heavenly Father. He's the one responsible for everything I have experienced in life and I thank Him every day for it all.

By the way, the show that night went great! It was a very emotional evening for me. I told the audience that too. I almost lost my composure on several songs. I never knew why, maybe it was because I knew I had lots of help that night and I was so grateful. If the audience enjoyed the show half as much as I did, then it was truly a successful night.

I got back into my bathroom after the show that night and in all my excitement over the show, I forgot to say thank-you to the one responsible. As I sat there, it all came back to me. The endless, "Dear Lord, help me through this night. Please help me remember all the words . . ." I just smiled and started singing "Oh! How I love Jesus"! Isn't it sweet that He's always around, in sickness and in health, for richer for poorer, and never, ever will we part.

Little Surprises Can Sure Mean a Lot

M*y daddy would not strike you* as a particularly expressive individual, let alone the real romantic type. But sometimes those quiet, gruff, sly old foxes can still surprise their ladies, and maybe that's one of the secrets behind my parents' nearly half-century marriage.

Now, my mama is one sharp lady, and she has always watched her husband with a keen eye and cut him very little slack. Still, just this past year, Daddy was able to pull a really sweet fast one on Mama.

They traveled over to San Angelo, Texas, to watch the steer-roping competitions. After the roping, Daddy took Mama to the steak house there in San Angelo for dinner. Now, every year Mama usually thinks about her birthday, whether she looks forward to it or dreads it. But she said this year there was too much going on for her to dwell on it much.

So, at the steak house they had a wonderful meal, and just about the time Mama thought they were finished and ready to leave, out came the surprise! During the meal Daddy had gotten up to go to the rest room and had talked to their waiter.

Out came a piece of apple caramel pie with a single lit candle on top of it.

If she had been expecting a huge, lavish birthday cake with seventy-three candles on top, that one piece of pie would have been a huge disappointment. But the beauty of it all was that Mama hadn't expected anything. And in return she received a very thoughtful gesture. Daddy was thinking of her and he took the time to arrange this small celebration. That touched her more than anything else he could have done.

Little things mean a lot.

When Narvel and I had been in Australia last spring for almost four weeks, I was getting really eager to see Shelby. He'd been with us the first week over in New Zealand and Australia but had flown back home so he wouldn't miss any more school. We had been e-mailing each other and I'd call him twice a day, but that wasn't as good as getting to hold him tight and kiss him!

So, on the day we landed back home safely in Tennessee, we carried all our luggage off the plane and loaded it in the Suburban that Kimmie had brought over for us to drive home. I was a little disappointed that Shelby wasn't there to meet us, but he might have had something else more important to do at home. When Narvel and I got in the front seat, I saw a note and a small bouquet of flowers there on the floorboard. The note said, "Dear Mom and Dad, *Welcome home!* Love, Shelby."

That got me! I was about to tear up, when I heard something in the very back seat. We looked around and up jumped Shelby! He was grinning from ear to ear! Boy, were we glad to see him! I asked Shelby, "How did you get here?"

And about that time Kimmie came walking out of the airport office. "I just knew you guys would see us when you flew in! We were trying to surprise you!" Kimmie said.

"Oh, we did!" Shelby said, laughing, still tickled that he'd gotten us.

Yes, little things can sure mean a lot. Kimmie is real good at thinking up things like that. It also makes it fun for Shelby to see his mama and daddy so happy to see him.

Once again the pleasure was even better because I didn't expect it.

* * *

I love to be surprised! It's a huge compliment that someone took the time and energy to do something that special for me.

I love to surprise others too!

Very often I'll get a phone call at the office informing me of someone's family member or friend being in the hospital either terminally ill or with a scheduled surgery coming up. I've even heard about someone being let out of the hospital with no hope and being sent home. Or maybe it's a little girl going for her next set of chemotherapy treatments.

My most recent call was from a friend asking me to phone a sixth-grade teacher who was going through chemotherapy on her birthday. I called as soon as I could. And when I talked to the young lady on the phone, I was truly surprised. She was very calm about the whole deal, and after I wished her a happy birthday she thanked me for calling. I thought to myself, Boy, would I be that collected and calm if I were in her place?

But what was so much of an eye-opener to me was that I had been so busy all day with details of my next CD, getting our pictures and videos in chronological order, autographing CDs that my record label, MCA, had sent over, and in a hurry to get home, and there she was in a hospital bed fighting for her life!

I then realized that making that one phone call was more important than any career project I had done all day. I hope it made her feel better. It sure did me.

So I guess we both got the surprise!

My Favorite Things in the World Are Memories

I *carry a camera with me everywhere* I go. One of my favorite things to do when I'm home is to sit and arrange my pictures in a photo album in chronological order, write in the captions, and at the same time revisit each place to which I've been. I also love to watch movies. I've learned a lot from films, whether it's history, geography, or just interesting information. I usually learn something, and I'm always entertained.

One Sunday afternoon before we had to leave for my show, Narvel, Chassidy, and I went to see a movie. Now, I'm the one who is a movie fanatic! Chassidy is second, and Narvel would rather sit at home or go have a root canal! Well, not that bad, but close. But on this day Narvel picked the Steven Spielberg movie *Saving Private Ryan.* I didn't want to go see it. It's a story about World War II, and we had friends who fought in that war. And it reminded me of last summer.

Last summer Narvel and I took Mama, Daddy, Brandon, Shelby, Garett, and Autumn on a European vacation with a cruise stuck in the middle of the three weeks. While we were in Italy we were going from Siena to Florence, when the tour guide pointed out the American cemetery from WW II. Mama immediately said she wanted to go in and visit it. Daddy said, "Well, we can just look at it as we drive by if no one else wants to go in." But Mama was adamant about it, I could tell, so I quickly agreed that it would be good for all of us to see it. While we were walking in and taking pictures at the entrance, the immense impact of where we were hit us. We were walking among heroes, among men and women who gave their lives for our country. If it weren't for them, we wouldn't have the freedom we live with and enjoy today.

I was doing the commentary with my video camera and then I focused it on Mama. She had tears streaming down her cheeks. I couldn't talk anymore. The lump in my throat was similar to the one I have in my throat right now. And when I looked at Daddy, it was worse.

We all walked in respectful silence, down the rows of crosses and Stars of David. We continued to take pictures by statues and grave markers. We read names on the markers, and in the visitors' center we read things that children and grandchildren had written about their fathers and grandfathers being left there in the cemetery. They commented on how clean and pretty it was and thanked whoever kept it so nice for doing so. It was quite moving.

I couldn't imagine how hard it would be to leave knowing one of your family members was left there, in another country, on foreign soil.

It was a quiet ride back to Florence and a day none of us will ever forget. When the trip was over, I had the job of getting all the pictures developed and distributed to Mama, Autumn, and Garett. When Mama and Daddy got their copies, Daddy took the pictures from our visit to the cemetery over to a good friend of ours, J. V. Newberry in Wardville, Oklahoma. J.V. had fought in Italy during WW II. Daddy told me later that J.V. said he wished that Daddy had never shown him the pictures. On one of the cross grave markers he saw the name of one of his buddies whom he had fought alongside during the war.

By the way, I thoroughly enjoyed the movie. It moved me. We were in the car for at least ten minutes before I could talk without crying.

But good or bad, my favorite things in the world are memories. Pictures help us remember and movies re-create things we might have never known. I hope one day I get to personally thank Steven Spielberg for making such a wonderful and moving memory, the movie *Saving Private Ryan.*

Funerals

I *was very surprised to learn that* a good friend of mine, Lori Turner, at the age of thirty-two, was about to attend her very first funeral. The reason I was so surprised was that I'd been going to funerals since I was a little girl. I had gone as a family member, I had gone as a friend, and I had sung at most of them.

One of the first funerals I remember singing at was for a very elderly lady, and it was held at the small church in Wardville, Oklahoma. Mama, Susie, Pake, and I were the singers for the funeral, and everything was going quite normally until we finished the second verse of the song we were singing. That's when Pake closed his hymnal and sat down. The rest of us continued on to the next verse, and Pake jumped up, trying to find his place in the songbook. You know how it is when you're in church and you're not supposed to laugh but that just makes it funnier? Well, the look on Pake's face took the cake! Susie and I were shaking, we were laughing so hard. Mama thought we were crying and reached around Pake and patted Susie on the shoulder. I knew if Mama had known that we were laughing at a funeral, she'd tan our hides! We did tell her years later.

There have been lots of friends of mine who have asked me to sing at their funerals when they die. What do you say when someone asks you that? I even told Connie Smith, after she had sung "How Great Thou Art" so movingly at Minnie Pearl's funeral, I'd die today if she'd sing at my funeral. She's always been my favorite!

She said, "Well, let's put it off awhile, okay?!"

I had spoken instead of singing at some friends' funerals when I knew I wouldn't be able to hold a note because of emotion. That's what happened when we lost Conway Twitty. They had asked me to sing at Conway's memorial service, but I told them I wouldn't be able to do that. I had toured with Conway for several years. I'd watched him, listened to him, and learned from him. But I asked if I could say a few things about Conway instead.

The main thing I wanted to say was how much I appreciated him for the good influence he had had on me throughout my career. I worked with Conway when he had the flu with a high temperature. He showed up at the venue and did a sound check before the show that night. I thought, My goodness, he's a superstar and he's going to sound check. It made me work harder because Conway did.

I never did get to tell Conway what a big fan of his I was and how he encouraged in me what my mama and daddy had instilled. I wish I had. They planted the seed and he set it a bit deeper. Then, as I looked out and saw Barbara Mandrell and the Statler Brothers, I was overwhelmed by a need to tell them right then and there of my deep gratitude to them. So I did, I thanked them for their help, their determination, and their inspiring commitment to give their fans their all. And I said if Dolly Parton had been there, I would have thanked her as well.

I did not want to miss this opportunity by letting another day go by without telling them how I felt. I loved opening the show for Conway. I sure do miss him.

Never put off till tomorrow what you can do today. That's one lesson I learned from losing my band members and tour manager in a 1991 plane crash. If you feel compelled to tell someone you love him or her or if you feel like giving someone a hug, *do it*! They probably need it as much as you do.

And *keep it up,* keep telling them and hugging them and making sure they hear and feel your love and friendship directly from you as often as you can.

Jim Clark, a good friend of the family's, told us one of his buddies was getting to be very despondent and was always depressed. He moped around all the time. He'd lost his zest for life.

One day Jim's friend came up to him, told Jim he was tired of living, and asked if Jim would be a pallbearer at his funeral. Now, if Jim's suspicions were accurate, his friend was thinking of taking his own life, and perhaps he could stop him. So Jim told him he didn't have time to go to any funeral, that he was too busy. Couldn't he put it off for a while? The friend said, "Okay," and went on home. Jim thought he had accomplished his mission. A year to the day later Jim's friend killed himself.

I attended Minnie Pearl's funeral. It was so sweet. There was a young lady playing the violin almost Appalachian style. She played all alone. Then Connie Smith sang "How Great Thou Art." That was my grandma's favorite song. I sat there looking up, wondering if Minnie was among us. I know she was happier and felt better than the last time I saw her. I had gone to see Minnie in the nicest nursing home I had ever been in. Her room was warm and cozy. Her closest friends' pictures were lovingly placed all around the room. I told her how pretty I thought it was, and she said, "It's a hellhole!" I could tell from that statement that she'd rather be anywhere but there. But it wasn't the room or the home, it was that Minnie wasn't free to get up and go like she'd done for so many years. She hated the confinement that her body and cancer had condemned her to.

I actually enjoyed her funeral. She was free. Free to fly, tell jokes, cut up, and dance. Just like in the good ol' days.

Then there was Mama Mae's funeral. Mama Mae, as she was known to everyone in the music business, was Mae Axton. She was the mother of Johnny Axton, who had been an attorney in Ada, Oklahoma, near my hometown, and Hoyt Axton, country singer, songwriter, and movie star. At her funeral, when I had gotten up to speak after a few people had already spoken, I said that I thought I was the only one who referred to Mae as "Mama Mae." Boy, was I wrong! Anyone who was close to Mae called her that. That's just the way she wanted it.

She had helped so many people in the business. She had even lent Elvis Presley money for a hotel room one time. She also wrote "Heartbreak Hotel" for Elvis. I asked Mae to go to a show with me, and at that time we were flying in a G-2, a Gulfstream 2. One of those big ol' planes! Oh, she loved that!

Well, a couple of weeks before, Lorianne Crook and Charlie Chase of the *Crook & Chase* TV show had leased our plane. When the catering was brought out, much to the pilot's embarrassment there were no forks in the pantry. Well, somehow Mae heard about this, and when our catering came out on our trip, Mae started digging in her purse. I looked over at her and she grinned that wonderful grin of hers and said, "I came prepared!" as she thrust this huge fork into the air like it was some kind of machete! When we arrived back in Nashville, we hugged good-bye and she climbed into the limo I had gotten for her to take her home. The remainder of the catering went with her too.

She asked me to bring Shelby over to see her one afternoon. After we got into the house, she took us downstairs, where her pool table was. She knew Shelby would like that. That's when she sat me down and told me the doctors thought she had cancer. As she told me this, I knew she expected me to break down and cry, but I had no sadness in my heart. I didn't think she had cancer. I don't know why, but I didn't. A few weeks later she called me and said that when she was in surgery and the doctors went in to remove the cancer, they didn't find anything. Mae later died peacefully in her home in Hendersonville, Tennessee. I sure do miss my Mama Mae.

When we were in Australia in the spring of 1998 touring with Kenny Rogers, I was getting off the plane in Sydney, when Darren from Universal Australia told me that Tammy Wynette had passed away. My mind went instantly to the last time I had seen Tammy. We were at an ASCAP writers' awards party in Nashville. I had gone to the ladies' room and was washing my hands, when someone elbowed me and said, "Hey, girl!" I looked over and saw Tammy. It had been a while since I had seen her, and I was shocked at how different she looked. Her face was soft and wrinkled like a beautiful handmade quilt. But the sparkle and fire were still in her eyes. We talked for a little while, then went back to our respective seats.

In 1984 I had shared a dressing room with Tammy, Emmylou Harris, and Brenda Lee. Tammy had told us she had had surgery that had taken out a large part of her stomach. She smiled and said she didn't have to eat nearly as much to get full nowadays! She always had a good way of looking at things!

That night in Sydney I did a telephone interview with a radio station in New York City about Tammy. As they had me on hold, they were playing an interview they had done with Tammy a few years before. Hearing her voice again, I got a big ol' lump in my throat. How come you don't know how much you miss them until they're gone? I called George Richey, Tammy's husband, soon after that and told him of the outpouring of love and respect everyone in Australia had for Tammy.

I didn't get to go to it, but I heard the funeral was beautiful, just like Tammy.

Roy Acuff, the king of country music, probably

had the best idea in the way of funerals. The news of his passing wasn't released until after he was already in the ground.

When we lost seven band members, Jim Hammon, my tour manager, and two pilots in the crash in 1991, I had asked Johnny Cash to speak at the memorial service. He said yes and did a wonderful job. It helped all of us to hear his words of wisdom and comfort. I have always admired Johnny for his strength to endure the hardships that life has put upon him. And his being there for us only strengthened my love for him. I found out later that his mother had just died the week before. He still said yes to us to help us through our grieving time even though he was in mourning for his mother.

Walking in the Sunshine

U*nfortunately, I know what it feels* like when tragedy strikes. I lost seven members of my band and my tour manager in a plane crash March 16, 1991. The pain of losing my friends so suddenly, so needlessly, was almost too much to bear.

But the way I see it, I had a choice: I could either walk in the sunshine or walk in the mud. It all depended on how I looked at life, and whether I could see some good behind the bad.

I wondered, why did this happen, why did the plane crash, why wasn't it my plane instead of theirs, and why did they have to die? I couldn't dwell on those terribly haunting but unanswerable questions. I had to stay centered for the families of those departed friends, for my organization, and for the fans.

I tried my best to prepare my heart for whatever it had to endure, and I struggled to go on.

That's what I mean by walking in the sunshine or walking in the mud. It was up to me to choose whether to be destroyed by this tragedy—and walk in the mud—or somehow to find a way to learn from it and grow stronger—and walk in the sunshine. I would not let my departed friends down. They expected me to handle a crisis when they were alive and I was certain they would expect no less from me now. We all had struggled together to succeed and overcome many obstacles together.

Nine days after the accident I was scheduled to perform "I'm Checking Out of This Heartbreak Hotel" (the song Meryl Streep sang in the movie *Postcards from the Edge)* at the Academy Awards. I remember, I kept hearing the lyrics in my head, and I wondered if the "heartbreak hotel" represented the world, and that my departed friends had "checked out" and were somewhere else, somewhere that was better.

I was back home in Nashville, sitting at my vanity the day after the crash, going over the song, trying to decide if I could sing it at the Oscar presentations, and suddenly a peaceful feeling swept over me. It was as if the band and Jim, my tour manager, were telling me to go on and sing the song. They were all right and they were still with me. I told Narvel I was going to perform the song as planned.

He said, "Are you sure?"

I said, "Yes, I'm sure. I'm gonna sing it for them."

I sang the song with all my heart. I was singing it for the friends I had lost. It was a very special performance for me. And I think the audience felt something very special as well. I know a few of them knew what had just happened and that I was suffering. It was like we were communicating with each other, and in the middle of so much grief I actually experienced precious moments filled with huge joy. I think that moment gave me the strength and confidence to go on.

The way I look at it, those few moments were a little good behind the bad, and I let them become a part of me the way the accident will always be a part of me. The first ray of sunshine, you could call it.

Yes, the crash was tragic and devastating. But I was comforted by my belief that everything happens for a reason. I might not know what the reason is, but that's not the important thing. The important thing, at least for me, was to believe with all my heart that they are definitely in a better place. And my job was to go on and continue with my music, for me and for them. I never questioned whether I should go on after that Oscar performance. My music was a tremendous consolation to me. It was something we had shared, and, in my mind, will share forever.

In the weeks that followed, I felt that I didn't want to be close to anyone ever again because I thought they too might be taken from me without warning. I think this is a normal feeling for someone who has lost someone dear to them. But I finally realized you can't live your life like that. Life is all about getting close, having relationships. Losing friends and family hurts deeply, but if you want to truly experience life, you have to learn to take both the good and the bad.

I did ask a very special favor of God. I asked Him to prepare my heart in case anything that devastating were to happen again. I didn't ask for bad things not to happen, I just asked Him to prepare me.

I know bad things can happen to anyone, but I also know that I can't control that. All I can do is face whatever bad things happen with all the strength and courage I can summon from within so that I can go on with my life. That in itself is the hardest thing any of us will ever have to do, but we have to do it.

Picking Myself Back Up

O*ur family, the year Shelby was* born, found a new family activity, snow skiing! No one in either Narvel's or my family had ever skied before, so we were excited and a little nervous about it. We first started our skiing experience in Crested Butte, Colorado, in December 1990. It was gorgeous!

It was a dream come true for me, because growing up in Oklahoma, we never saw a white Christmas. It was cold and icy but hardly ever snowed! The same was true for Narvel growing up in Texas. Narvel, Shawna, Brandon, Chassidy, and I all started out together on the bunny slopes with lessons while Shelby and Cindy Bailey, Shelby's nanny at the time, settled into our hotel room for a week of wintertime bliss. It started a tradition we all loved.

After Crested Butte we moved the next year over

to Aspen! We rented a beautiful log cabin for two weeks and again had a wonderful time! The next year we again moved next door to Snowmass Mountain after finding a house that fit our growing family even better. It was so much fun having friends like Ralph and Joy Emery and Barbara Mandrell and her husband, Ken Dudney, and all their kids over. We had a great time. We skied every year, and all of us were improving slowly but surely.

Then, right after Thanksgiving in 1996, Narvel, Sandi Spika, and I flew to Salt Lake City, Utah, and drove up to Park City for a little layover time before our show Tuesday night in Salt Lake. Sandi, Scott Borchetta, VP of national promotion of MCA Records at the time, Bill Mackey, the West Coast regional promotion man for MCA, Narvel, and I hit the slopes bright and early on Monday morning. We skied all day and had a great dinner that night. The next day we hit the slopes again, until we had to stop and go down to Salt Lake for my show.

I was touring with Billy Dean that year. It was the most elaborate, theatrical, eventful, moving show I'd ever done. I was more proud of this year's show than any year before. I had ten dancers with me and our stage was from one end of the arena floor to the other. The stage was in the center of the arena with runways going to opposite ends of the main stage, one end having an octagon stage and the other end having a rectangular stage. They had devised for me a small mechanical arm that would pull a riser from one end of the arena to the other. We set up a scene for "Is There Life Out There?" on the moving riser for Betsy, one of my dancers, to ride on and play the part of the lady in the song. During another part of the performance we showed a short video about Mama and Daddy. Then I'd come out from changing clothes and get on the moving riser with Doug Sisemore, my piano player and bandleader. I'd sing "The Greatest Man I Never Knew" going down the runway and after the chorus, Jennifer Wrinkle, my fiddle player, would walk toward me on the opposite runway and play the fiddle solo. While she was doing that, I would walk to the center of the main stage and finish the song there.

Now, back while the video was playing, my crew were placing a heavy piece of material on the center stage. So when I got through with "The Greatest Man," I was standing center stage in the middle of this material. When "She Thinks His Name Was John" started, the small square in the center of the stage took me up into the air about eight feet. The material was attached and it came up with me. On the last verse, lights from above shone down on the material and it became the AIDS quilt. I'm glad I couldn't see the whole effect. I probably wouldn't have been able to sing. It was a very moving part of the show. I could go on and on about that show. It was my favorite.

So, on the night of our show in Salt Lake, once again I had a great time. I changed clothes nine times during the show, six times less than the year before. And after skiing all day and doing a very physical show, I was pooped! We drove back to Park City after the show, and again the next morning, all of us were on the slopes, ready to ski.

I noticed on the first run down the mountain the effects of skiing the last two days and performing a show. My legs were tired. I didn't have as much energy as the day before. So when we stopped for lunch, I was debating on whether to quit early and head back to the lodge or keep going. I kept going. But finally I told Narvel, "Let me have the keys to the van. I'm going on down and I'll wait for y'all there." He said, "Well, I'm getting pretty tired too. Let's just ski this last run and then I'll go in with you."

Everyone agreed to that, so off we went. Going down the mountain, we made it off the blues and were on the green runs, which are the easiest. The sun was already behind the mountain, casting shadows on the snow. That's when it's always harder for me to see. I need the sun to show me the dips and contours of the hill. I had been skiing better on this trip than ever before. I was tickled to death. I was finally getting my speed up to where it was easier to ski and felt less pressure on my legs. I was having lots of fun. It would have been the best if I hadn't been so tired.

On that run down I had let everyone else go first. I guess I wanted to see if I could catch up with them, since I was finally skiing faster. Just as I was skiing around Sandi, my ski hit an icy edge in the snow, which caused me to lose control. Because of my fatigue, I couldn't pull my skis back together, so down I went. My bindings didn't release like they were supposed to. They were going back and forth like windshield wipers. I heard the pop. I didn't know what it was, but I knew it was something serious.

When I finally stopped, Sandi was there immediately with Bill right behind her. Narvel and Scott were already down the hill too far to see what had happened. Then there was a person from the rescue unit skiing toward us. He asked me some questions, put a box of Kleenex under my head, and together we determined that I had hurt my left leg. We didn't know how badly, I just knew it hurt to move it. I didn't think it was broken, but something was not right. Bill suggested that either he or Sandi should ski down and let Narvel and Scott know what had happened. Sandi didn't budge! She wasn't going anywhere! That's a true friend! I lay there on the snow, thinking, What on earth have I done? How is this going to affect the rest of my life? Sandi started talking to me, trying to lighten up the moment. It helped. I never cried, it didn't hurt that bad at the time. I was just curious about the extent of the damage. The man who had stopped to help us radioed for someone to bring a sled down. And not too long after that there came a snowmobile with a sled behind it. They put me in the sled and pulled me down the mountain. Halfway down the slope the sled was transferred from the snowmobile to a person on skis, who took me down the rest of the way to the first aid center.

When I saw Narvel it made me feel a lot better. I knew he'd take care of everything. I was worried most about their having to take my ski boot and ski suit off. I knew that was going to pull on my leg and it was going to hurt! I was dreading that! But they were very gentle. They took X rays of my leg and the doctor said I had broken not a bone but the spine off my tibia. That was pure Greek to me! He also said I should go down to University Hospital in Salt Lake, have an MRI done, and get a second opinion.

So Narvel, Sandi, Scott, and Bill loaded me up in the backseat of the Explorer and Narvel drove me down to the hospital. On our way down Narvel and I were discussing how we would alter the show with my leg being hurt. We were changing the show list around, putting me on a chair that swiveled with a support mechanism for my leg to rest on. There was nothing that couldn't be handled. I wasn't in that much pain, so we thought I'd be able to go on and do my show the next day. *Wrong!*

After Dr. Burks at University Hospital examined my leg and looked at the results of the CAT scan they had taken, he explained the damage. I had indeed broken the spine off the tibia inside my knee. The best way I can explain it is my shin and thigh went in opposite directions and caused the muscle that goes through the knee to pop off the bone above the knee. When that happened, the muscle took a part of the bone with it.

Narvel wanted to know if we could finish the eight shows we had left on the tour and then come back to Salt Lake, do the operation, and fix it. But after Dr. Burks had pulled and tugged on my leg, I said, "Absolutely not!" It felt like I had a piece of gravel inside my knee! I wanted it fixed! And I wanted it fixed then and there! So they took me to a hospital room and got me ready for surgery. That's all I remember about that! Those knockout drugs worked very well on me!

The next morning Dr. Burks said the surgery had gone well and I could go back to Park City. Narvel was glad, because the weather was getting worse in Salt Lake. While we were waiting for all the procedures to be taken care of, they told me that Terri Clark, another female country artist, had called to see how I was. I asked, "Did she leave a number?"

I called Terri back and thanked her for thinking of me. That was the best medicine I could have taken. It means a lot to me to have friends. I hadn't been around Terri that much, but since then we've made up for lost time. Terri was on our 1998 tour with Brooks & Dunn, David Kersh, and me. We had a blast! She is so out there! She'd come over to my dressing room after her show and we'd swap stories about the business, what's going right and what's going wrong. Not that either one of us could fix the other one's problems, but it's nice to be able to *vent* every once in a while!

The doctors released me from the hospital and we went back to Park City. By that time my epidural was wearing off and I was hurting really bad! Narvel kept the cold water flowing through the special knee brace they had given me. It helped keep the swelling down. I think I almost put Narvel's back out of place from all the times he had to help me to the bathroom, getting me in and out of the bed.

During the night I threw up, and by morning I was hurting so badly that even thinking about doing my show that night would make me hurt even more! So Narvel called Brian Leedham, my production manager, and Trey Turner, my promoter, and let them know we were canceling the weekend shows. The crew was already at the venue putting the show up when Trey and Brian told them the news.

Linda Davis, my duet partner, who was with me on tour, told me later: "It sure was a weird feeling. We didn't know how bad off you were. We didn't feel that they were telling us the whole story, so that made it even worse. All of us were worried sick about you! When you didn't make the show in Tucson, we drove on to Phoenix, hoping you'd be okay to do that show. But like I said, we just didn't know!"

I tried not to think of all the people we had out on the road, ready to work, ready to get the show up and running. I tried not to think about them sitting in hotel rooms for six days, waiting for the phone call telling them whether or not I would be able to do the next scheduled show. Any person in their right mind would have said "Okay, that's it for the year! Thanks so much! We had fun!"

But, oh, no! Not us! We adjusted. We made it to where the show could go on. We made plans to stay at the hotel in Park City that weekend until my next show in San Jose, California, that next Tuesday. Since we weren't working, Narvel flew Shelby, Garett, and Brandon out to be with us. That made me feel a lot better! I was missing Shelby so badly and Narvel knew it. It also helped to take my mind off my leg.

It seemed like a good idea at the time, but the next day they all went skiing, and Garett, having skied just once before, skied off the trail and ended up in a grove of trees. She almost dislocated her shoulder and bent her thumb back. You can imagine my surprise when Narvel brought Shelby to the room saying he had to go back to the first aid center to check on Garett! Skiing was becoming a dreaded word about that time! We were all relieved that Garett wasn't hurt any more than she was. The kids went back to Nashville on Sunday night, and on Tuesday I made the scary trip to San Jose. I have the utmost respect for the physically impaired. Having restrictions on what you can do, when you can do it, if you can do it is the most irritating, confusing, frustrating, aggravating, cruel thing I have ever experienced! And the physically impaired folks deal with this every day. Ever since my recovery, when I go into a public rest room, I won't use the handicap toilet even if it's the only one available and there's not a physically impaired person in the room. First of all, I know how it feels to need to use that one specially built stall and finding it occupied by someone it wasn't designed for. And I'm so deeply grateful that I don't have to use it anymore that I stay away from it! I won't let my kids use it either. It's meant for the ones who need it! No one else! The same goes for parking spaces. I wouldn't even think of parking in a handicap parking space. Getting into the car, out of the car, and into the plane was something I had never thought twice about. But with a hurt knee, we were all thinking! I had to have a special chair brought for me to sit in while they pulled and carried me into our plane.

When we got to the venue for sound check, we put my wheelchair on the riser, set my brakes, the band started playing, and I began rehearsing with my dancers. So while the riser was moving down the runway, I was singing and the dancers were dancing all around me, when all of a sudden the riser came to an abrupt stop! That jerked me forward and then flung me back, which caused my chair to fall over backward.

But it stopped in midair!

I thought Terry, one of my dancers, had caught me. I said to myself, "Whew!" But about that time, over I went, on my back, with my hurt leg straight in the air! Over my microphone I said, *"This is never going to work!"*

At the same time, Narvel leaned over to Ricky Moeller, my house sound engineer, and said, "Turn her microphone off." I guess because of the mental state I was in and what I'd been through, he wasn't sure what I might say next. He was right. I had about lost it. I couldn't see any way in the world that the show was gonna go on without a hitch. Those people were used to seeing me dance and change clothes nine to fifteen times in a show. What were they going to do when I showed up in a wheelchair and just sang? It was very nerve-racking getting ready for the show that night. Things were different. For me, nothing was the same. But, as usual, the band and dancers were right on. On the dance numbers I constantly worried about one of them hitting my leg while they ran and danced around me. My crew worked extra hard to make sure everyone was in the right place at the right time. But still I worried that me not being able to dance into my mark, I wouldn't remember the words to my songs. I was a creature of habit. I relied on repetition to get me from song to song. But even after the first song, when the audience saw I wasn't going to do anything more than sing, they stayed. They didn't leave. They came to hear me sing. It's weird that no matter how much success you achieve, no matter how secure you think you are, insecurity can hit you the hardest when you least expect it. I had been selling out arenas. Almost every venue sells out the day we put the tickets on sale. But still, I wondered if tonight they would stay or walk out.

Song after song, I slowly remembered why I chose this profession. I sat there in the chair, singing. Not dancing, not walking, not running from one end of the stage to the other, and not running back to the quick-change area to once again put on another outfit. I just sang the songs, from my heart, with as much passion as I had to offer. I fell in love with the music all over again. And I once again remembered why I love this job so much!

I Know I'll Have a Better Day Tomorrow

In *the early '80s I wrote* and recorded a song in which I tried to convey my faith, my gratitude, and my belief that the best in life can still be in tomorrow's hours. "I Know I'll Have a Better Day Tomorrow" has become only more meaningful to me over the years.

> I can't make it through this world by myself,
> I need Heaven's help to make it through the
>   day.
> If I go to bed tonight and remember to say
>   my prayers
> I know I'll have a better day tomorrow.
>
> You've done what You said You'd do,
> And You've given me lots of love,

I've never known such peace since I met You.
I'm so proud to be Your child,
And I'm doing the best I can,
And I know I'll have a better day tomorrow.

For all the latest news about Reba and *Comfort From a Country Quilt* as well as highlights from her tour, plus all the newest photos, be sure to log on to Reba's website: www.reba.com.